Five-Minute Mini-Mysteries

Stan Smith

Illustrated by Kathleen O'Malley

Sterling Publishing Co., Inc.
New York

Dedicated with love to Julie, our daughter Jennifer,
our son Benjamin, and in memory of baby Carolyn

"Crime is common. Logic is rare. Therefore it is upon the logic, rather than
upon the crime, that you should dwell."

—*Sherlock Holmes*

Library of Congress Cataloging-in-Publication Data

Smith, Stan (Stanley E.)
    Five-minute mini-mysteries / Stan Smith ; illustrated by Kathleen
O'Malley.
        p.   cm.
    Includes index.
    ISBN 1-4027-0031-8
    1. Puzzles. 2. Detective and mystery stories. I. Title.
GV1507.D4 S52   2002
793.73—dc21

                                        2002151753

20 19 18 17

Published by Sterling Publishing Co., Inc.
387 Park Avenue South, New York, NY 10016
© 2003 by Stanley Smith
Distributed in Canada by Sterling Publishing
ᶜ/o Canadian Manda Group, 165 Dufferin Street
Toronto, Ontario, Canada M6K 3H6
Distributed in Great Britain and Europe by Chris Lloyd at Orca Book
Services, Stanley House, Fleets Lane, Poole BH15 3AJ, England
Distributed in Australia by Capricorn Link (Australia) Pty. Ltd.
P.O. Box 704, Windsor, NSW 2756, Australia

Manufactured in the United States of America
All rights reserved

Sterling ISBN-13: 978-1-4027-0031-6
        ISBN-10: 1-4027-0031-8

For information about custom editions, special sales, premium and
corporate purchases, please contact Sterling Special Sales
Department at 800-805-5489 or specialsales@sterlingpub.com.

Contents

Introduction

WELCOME, FRIENDS OLD and new of Thomas P. Stanwick, to a new collection of solve-it-yourself mystery puzzles to amuse you and exercise your mind!

Readers of the two previous collections of Stanwick mystery puzzles, *Five-Minute Whodunits* and *Five-Minute Crimebusters*, will be pleased to learn that the amateur logician and his black Lab, Rufus, are still contentedly ensconced in the small New England town of Baskerville. Join Stanwick once again as he helps Inspector Walker of the Royston Police, Inspector Bodwin of Scotland Yard, and Logic Club friends Amanda Tucker and Susan Carlie untangle crimes and other mysteries.

In this collection you will find a smorgasbord of crime that includes murder, robbery, kidnapping, arson, smuggling, and forgery. In a more innocent vein, a sprinkling of practical logic problems involving such items as scholarships, travel plans, and farm animals are included as well. Baskerville, Royston, London, and the puzzling English village of Knordwyn, the home of invet-

5

erate liars and truthtellers, are among the places where Stanwick does his deducing.

As previous Stanwick readers are aware, these mystery puzzle collections combine elements of the traditional whodunit (physical clues, red herrings, means, motive, opportunity, time sequences) with those of straightforward logic problems (true-false statements, matching suspects with occupations, even a little math here and there). Not knowing just what sort of puzzle each story will contain is part of the challenge to the reader.

Short mystery puzzles like these entertain you while giving your brain an agreeable workout in observant reading, visualization, logical deduction, and spotting inconsistencies in statements or physical circumstances. Each is self-contained and takes only, oh, five minutes or less to read. And they are suitable for both adults and bright children.

Most of all, mystery puzzles are fun! So whether you read these to solve them or simply to take in their glimpses of small town life (or even Stanwick's friendly banter)—do enjoy them.

The Case of the Suspicious Fire

SHORTLY AFTER THREE in the morning, Royston firefighters brought the fire at James Fine Clothing under control. Inspector Matthew Walker, who was on call that June night, squinted his eyes against the flashing red lights and drifting water spray that mingled with the voices of the firefighters. Patrolman Ryder saw the inspector and came up to him.

"The fire captain called Jerry James, the store owner, sir," he said. "Had to leave a message on his machine. The adjacent buildings are safe now, but everything in the store is destroyed."

Walker knew the store had been struggling in recent years, and suspected that the fire might be opportune.

"Who called the fire in?" he asked.

"Jimmy and I did, sir. We were on patrol nearby when it started."

"Did you see anyone in the area earlier?"

"Only one at this time of night, sir. A man with a brown beard wearing a cap and a knapsack. Light jacket and dark jeans. About five-ten in height. He was walking about a block from the store."

"Toward the store or away?"

"Away. We spotted the fire about fifteen minutes later."

"All right. Take a swing around and see if you spot him."

Ryder hurried off just as a fire captain approached Walker with a bleary-eyed, balding man. Walker knew Captain Henning.

"Walker, this is Jerry James, the owner of the store," Henning said. "He got my message and just arrived. I've briefed him on our progress."

"Thanks, Henning." Walker turned to James. "Mr. James, I understand the captain had to leave a message on your machine. Were you away from home?"

"No, Inspector," James replied distractedly. "I keep my bedside phone ringer switched off. Telemarketers have been disturbing my midday nap lately. I didn't hear the kitchen phone ring, but when I came back from using the bathroom I saw the message light of the bedside phone on. After listening to the captain's message, I threw on some clothes and rushed here."

"Is your store insured?" Walker asked casually.

"Yes, but it's been my life!"

"Any idea how the fire started?"

"No, none." James stared at the blaze. As he did, Walker discreetly examined his face for traces of glue that might have supported a false beard, but James's smooth, clean face revealed nothing. Walker did observe that his socks were mismatched. After asking James for his address, Walker calculated that he would not have had time to set the fire, go home to get the phone message, and return to the scene.

The inspector then turned to watch the dwindling fire, lost in weary thought.

"You usually play rook-and-pawn endings well, Matt," remarked Thomas P. Stanwick two evenings later. He and Walker settled themselves in the lounge of the Royston Chess Club after their weekly game. "That's to your credit, too, for they're one of the purest tests of chess skill. Tonight, though, you fell apart quickly. Anything on your mind?"

"Just tired," replied Walker. "I was at a fire downtown the other night."

"Oh, sure, always some excuse." Stanwick smiled. "You were sick. You had the black pieces. You were up all night investigating a crime."

"We don't know for sure that it was a crime," said Walker. "Do you know of James Fine Clothing?"

"Been in there. The clothing is a bit too fine for my taste."

"Obviously. Well, apparently a lot of other slobs agree with you. The place has had some financial problems, and I've learned that the fire occurred at a convenient time. The owner's creditors were starting to close in." Walker described the events and his observations of the evening.

"The fire department thinks arson is possible," he continued. "A wall panel near some electrical wiring had been removed. The insurance company is suspicious, though I suppose they always are. James has some electrical training, and he's the right height and hair color to fit the description of the bearded man the patrol saw in the area shortly before the fire started. But he lives too far away to have started the fire and made the round trip home for the phone message."

"Are you sure he heard the phone message?" asked Stanwick.

"Yes. I'm told that when he arrived at the fire, he referred to it and asked for Henning by name."

Stanwick idly fingered the tip of his drooping mustache.

"I would say," he offered, "that the insurance company's suspicions are well founded. James could indeed have set the fire. Not only is it possible, his story is certainly false, which makes his guilt probable. And despite the aspersions you cast on my wardrobe, I might, being the forgiving fellow I am, be willing to explain how I know."

How does Stanwick know that James is lying?

Solution on page 87.

Some Trouble at Harrigan's

WHEN THOMAS P. STANWICK, the amateur logician, stepped into Harrigan's Hardware Store in Baskerville shortly after eight one morning, he found its calm routine disrupted. Harrigan was pacing the floor in agitation, his face flushed, almost as red as his handlebar whiskers. Bob Lasketter, the senior shop clerk, and Fred Barrows, the junior assistant, stood nearby, pale and nervous.

"I'm sorry, Mr. Stanwick," said Harrigan, coming up to him, "but we can't help you right now. We've been robbed, and the police are on the way."

Stanwick raised his eyebrows. "Really? When? Just now?"

"Last night." Harrigan turned to Lasketter. "Everything was all right when you closed up last night, wasn't it, Bob?"

"Yes, sir," Lasketter replied. "I closed up at seven. Nothing unusual."

"And what happened this morning?" asked Stanwick.

"Bob and I unlocked and opened the store about half an hour ago," said Barrows. "While I turned on the register, Bob went to the office in back. He clicked on the light, and then kind of froze in the doorway and called out to me that the safe had been opened and the cash tray was gone. I went to check around the rest of the store while he came back and called Mr. Harrigan, who wasn't due in for another hour. I found the back door to the storage room forced open, but nothing seemed to be missing except the cash tray from the office safe. It had about six hundred dollars."

"That's right," interrupted Harrigan. "I came right over after Bob called, checked the place myself, and then called the police. That was just a few minutes ago."

"I guess I can buy my wrench later. I have a police pass," said Stanwick, opening his wallet to show it. "Do you mind if I have a quick look around? I won't disturb anything."

"Certainly, go ahead." Harrigan cleared his throat and resumed his pacing.

Stanwick strode to the office and looked in. A large, shabby desk dominated the center of the room. The gray metal cabinets and dusty shelves along the walls were covered with parts manuals, papers, and odd bolts and bits. To the right of the door, facing the desk, stood a three-foot-high safe. Stanwick walked to the desk, examined it quickly, and then went to the safe. Its door was swung partly open to his right, and its aged padlock, jimmied open, lay on the floor before him. Inside the safe were two compartments, the bottom still full of papers, and the top, which had held the cash tray, now empty.

Touching nothing, Stanwick left the office and entered the back storage room. Skirting several crates and lawnmowers, he approached and examined the back door, which was also partly open. The simple lock had been forced, and the surrounding wood was cracked. Stanwick quickly returned to the front of the shop.

"Most interesting," he remarked to no one in particular.

"I think I hear the police arriving," said Harrigan.

"Excellent," said Stanwick. "When the officer comes in," he continued, turning suddenly to Lasketter, "I hope you will tell him the truth. You committed this theft yourself!"

Why did Stanwick suspect Lasketter of the theft?

Solution on page 87.

An Evening with the Logic Club

THE MEMBERS OF the Logic Club were well into their monthly dinner, which was being held at the Shanghai Blossom restaurant in Royston. Present as usual were Thomas P. Stanwick; Inspector Walker of the Royston police; retired trial lawyer Whit Knowlton; Regis Arnold, a philosophy professor at Royston State; attorney Amanda Tucker; and Susan Carlie, a statistician for a state agency.

A friendly debate over the legitimacy of the fourth figure of the categorical syllogism had come to an unexpected pause. Carlie realized that a change from theoretical to recreational logic was needed.

"My husband George and I," she said brightly, "were traveling some months ago in Gromoria. Our guide one night took us to a meeting of the Irrelevant Club."

"An irrelevant club?" asked Walker.

"*The* Irrelevant Club," said Carlie. "A social and educational club with rules based on irrelevant physical characteristics. It began as a joke years ago, but has really caught on over there. Members meet on the first and third Monday of the month to listen to music, a reading, or a lecture, or to play games, or just chat and have a snack."

Stanwick dabbed some sweet-and-sour sauce from his mustache.

"And what, my dear Sue," he asked, "are these curiously based rules of theirs?"

"Well, they group themselves by hair color, eye color, handedness, and whether or not they have pierced ears or appendectomy scars. Each blue-eye brings a bottle of wine to the second meeting of the month and recites a poem at the first. Each blonde brings cookies to the first meeting and a board game to the second. Pierced-ears each sing a song at the first meeting and bring a newsletter article to the second. Every leftie must bring cards to the first meeting. All black-eyes play a banjo at the second.

"Each brownhead brings a guest lecturer to either meeting," she continued. "Every scar-bearer brings doughnuts to the second meeting. Each redhead recites a short essay then as well. Each rightie brings either a board game, cards, or a poem to the first meeting or cookies to the second. To avoid strain, however, no one who brings something to recite may perform musically at the same evening."

"Pah!" exclaimed Knowlton. "I never could abide strange clubs."

"Unfortunately, Whit," said Carlie, "the rules pose a possible contradiction for Marta, a friend of our guide. She may have to resign from the club because of them."

"Why?" asked Tucker.

Carlie smiled. "That's for you to tell me. If you can. I'll take questions."

"Have the rules of this club always been strictly enforced?" asked Walker.

"Always. Violation means instant expulsion."

"Do members change their hair color, or even their eye color with contact lenses?" asked Knowlton.

"No."

"Since handedness and other qualities overlap, do members have to obey all rules that pertain to them?" asked Stanwick.

"Yes. Ambidextrous people, though, are considered neither righties nor lefties."

"All right, everyone," said Stanwick, grinning and tapping his water glass with his knife. "Deductions, please."

"Well," said Arnold, rubbing his smooth double chin, "Marta's eyes are not green or brown."

"And she probably had or was expecting a major birthday or anniversary," added Tucker.

"Correct, are they not, Sue?" remarked Stanwick.

"Quite correct, Tom," replied Carlie with a smile.

Why might Marta have to resign from the Irrelevant Club?

Solution on page 87.

The River War Robbery

CHIEF WILLIAM RYAN of the Baskerville Police was sitting on his front porch one unusually mild Sunday afternoon with Thomas P. Stanwick, the amateur logician. Stanwick's black Labrador, Rufus, slept lightly beside his master's wicker chair.

"Still working on a schoolbook, Tom?" asked the laconic Ryan.

"That's right, Bill," Stanwick replied. "I'm editing a textbook on American history from 1900–1950. It's a fascinating period."

"Don't I know it!" snorted Ryan. "I lived through most of it. Fought in World War Two. Are FDR and Churchill in the book? You never know, these days."

"Their names come up." Stanwick grinned.

"Say, you're particularly interested in Churchill, aren't you?"

"I am indeed. Why?"

"A book by Churchill was stolen from Fred Morgan's study three nights ago," said Ryan. "*The River War*, it was called. Morgan's a military historian who collects Churchill items. He says it was valuable."

Stanwick's eyes glistened. "Two volumes, dark blue, with a gilded riverboat illustration and author's signature on the covers?"

"Yes." Ryan looked at Stanwick suspiciously.

Stanwick whistled. "A first edition!" he exclaimed. "Very rare and worth several thousand, according to Langworth's guidebook. Please tell me more."

"Morgan has a large study on the ground floor," said Ryan. "Quite a room: high shelves, ceiling beams, heraldic banners. The thief forced entry at ten P.M. through a window by smashing the glass and pulling the bolt. A chair by the window was overturned, and the flowerbed outside was trampled. Some muddy marks were left on the hardwood floor, but no distinguishable prints. No fingerprints either. He grabbed the book and left as he came. Morgan discovered the theft the next morning."

"No one heard the glass break?"

"No. Morgan lives alone and was out at a Churchill dinner in Royston."

"Ah, yes. The Churchill Society was celebrating the great man's birthday. I was too busy to go myself. Any leads?"

Ryan took a sip of iced tea. "Only one, really," he replied. "The book was kept behind a sliding panel on the bookshelves. Not obvious. Nothing else was taken. Whoever took it must have known where to find it. Other than Morgan himself, only three people knew this. Peter Costello, a rival Churchill collector, viewed Morgan's collection two years ago. Stephen Grecco, a book dealer in Milverton, helped Morgan make an inventory of his collection several months ago. Morgan's former research assistant, Lynne Heffernan, left his employment shortly after the inventory was finished."

"Interesting." Stanwick relit his pipe. "I think I know Costello. About sixty, ruddy face, white hair, no glasses, bad teeth?"

"That's the one."

"What's his alibi?"

"Says he attended the same dinner as Morgan. He arrived late, just as the crowd was going in to dinner, and sat at a table near the exit. Morgan doesn't remember seeing him, but it was a crowded event, and they didn't look for each other. Costello tried to buy

The River War when he visited Morgan, and got very angry when Morgan turned him down. They haven't spoken since."

"How about the other two?"

"Grecco says he was home that evening watching TV with his wife. A cable news channel was doing a report on a tomato festival in Wisconsin when he dozed off shortly before eleven. Miss Heffernan says she was in the library stacks at Royston State, working on her doctoral thesis on Central African military tactics. No witnesses, though. She was in one of those private booths reserved for Ph.D. students."

"Why did she leave Morgan's employ?" asked Stanwick.

"She would only say that they parted on bad terms. Morgan said she was unreliable."

"Hmm. Why did Morgan have an inventory done, anyway?"

"He said he needed to update his insurance. The insurance investigator has found no evidence of fraud, though."

Rufus lifted his head and yawned. Stanwick languidly stood up and zipped his jacket.

"Well, Bill," he said, "I'd better get Rufus home for his supper. We enjoyed the visit. If I may, I'd like to repay your hospitality by pointing out the identity of the thief."

Who stole *The River War*?

Solution on page 88.

Murder in the Gallery

THE NATIONAL PORTRAIT Gallery was a favorite London haunt of Thomas P. Stanwick, the amateur logician. But not today. Not with a bloody body at his feet and a Scotland Yard inspector by his side.

Stanwick was starting a long July vacation. While in London for a few days, he had called on his burly friend Inspector Bodwin at New Scotland Yard. Bodwin, about to leave to visit a crime scene, had invited Stanwick along. Now they stood before the magnificent John Singer Sargent portrait of Ellen Terry as Lady MacBeth.

Lying at the foot of the portrait was a middle-aged man in a flowery shirt and casual slacks. He lay on his back in a puddle of blood, his short salt-and-pepper beard reddened from a long gash at his throat. Though blood spotted the wall, the portrait itself had been spared.

A police sergeant approached Bodwin.

"This is Harry Rosenthal, 58, a Yank tourist," the sergeant reported. "The lady standing over there, Laurel Rudd, befriended him on their tour and was visiting the gallery with him."

"Did she find the body?" asked Bodwin.

"No, one of the guards did. Miss Rudd said she had left Rosenthal near here to visit the loo. We have found no witness to the killing, but as you can see this is a small side room, and visitor traffic is light today."

Bodwin strode over to Laurel Rudd, a dignified woman in her late forties. "What can you tell me, Miss Rudd?"

"Nothing, I'm sure, Inspector," she replied wanly. "I met Harry on the flight over, and we were spending the free day in London together. The tour moves on tomorrow to Bath."

"Did Mr. Rosenthal mention any threats?"

"No, none. He lived quietly as a lighting technician at a TV station in Kenosha, Wisconsin. He had retired from the Marines as a captain when he was forty. His wife died several years ago."

"Where else have you two been today?"

"Just some shopping on the Strand. We were meeting a school friend of his for lunch at the Trafalgar Pub. Why, he's probably waiting there now!"

"Who is this friend?"

"His name is Jim Prichard, as I recall. He and Harry were in the high school drama club together. They hadn't seen each other since a high school reunion twenty years ago. Harry wanted to find a familiar face in London. This was before he met me. The high school alumni office found that Jim was living here. He's an architect, and has been posted over here for some while."

"So he was meeting Rosenthal in the Trafalgar," said Bodwin. "How would they recognize each other after all this time?"

"Oh, Harry was wearing his SPEBSQSA cap. It's—it's lying over there."

"SPEBSQSA?"

"The Society for the Preservation and Encouragement of Barbershop Quartet Singing in America," Stanwick cut in. "An outfit headquartered in Kenosha."

"I see." Bodwin stared at Stanwick for a moment to see if he were kidding, and decided he was not. "And how was Rosenthal to recognize Prichard?"

"Jim was going to wear a 'Manchester United' button on his collar."

A few minutes later, Stanwick and Bodwin were at the Trafalgar Pub. They quickly found a casually dressed man in his late fifties sitting at a secluded table and wearing the button.

"Yes, I'm Jim Prichard," he said. "What can I do for you gentlemen?"

"I'm Bodwin of the Yard, and this is Mr. Stanwick," said Bodwin. "We've just come from the portrait gallery, where a Harry Rosenthal was found dead. Throat cut. His companion said he was meeting you here for lunch today."

"Harry dead!" Prichard half rose from his seat and then sat back down heavily. "Yes, I was expecting him here anytime now. Hadn't seen each other for twenty years, so he was to wear a special cap. I'm wearing this button for him to spot."

"How did you two arrange this meeting, sir?" asked Stanwick.

"We exchanged telegrams. Old-fashioned, I know. The high school office gave him my London address, and he wanted to get together. Throat cut! I suppose he still kept his beard trim—too bad he didn't let it grow. Might have impeded the knife."

"So you were old friends?" Bodwin asked.

"Through high school, yes. Then we lost touch, except for the twentieth reunion and now. Poor Harry! Who was his companion? His wife?"

"No, a fellow tour member. Mr. Rosenthal was a widower."

"Poor Harry."

Stanwick took Bodwin aside.

"Odd, Gil, that he should pick a secluded table when he knows someone will be looking for him," he remarked.

Bodwin shrugged. "Perhaps the bar was already full."

"Perhaps. I would nonetheless suggest that you check his car trunk and the gallery men's room."

"Beg pardon?"

"Sorry. The boot of his car and the gents' loo."

"For what?"

"Bloody clothes, of course, and perhaps the knife if he is over-confident. And hold him."

"On what grounds?" Bodwin scoffed. "His choice of table?"

"No, no," Stanwick laughed. "More than that, I assure you."

Why did Stanwick suspect Prichard?

Solution on page 88.

The Harland Avenue Syndicate

THOMAS P. STANWICK and Inspector Matt Walker sat in comfortable armchairs beside a blazing hearth. This Thursday evening found them as usual in the lounge of the Royston Chess Club. While Walker moodily chewed on his cheap cigar, Stanwick blew leisurely clouds of smoke from his Calabash pipe.

"Your rook maneuver was quite unorthodox, Matt," Stanwick remarked contentedly, "but even with best play it couldn't save the endgame."

"Maybe not," grumped Walker, "but it's been a long week, and I'm tired."

"When will I ever convince you of the restorative powers of an afternoon nap?" Stanwick grinned at his friend. "Churchill never missed his, and he carried a war."

"I'm not the one who needs convincing. Tell the chief. If he found me napping, he'd bust me down to traffic cop."

"Come, come. Next time you stop at a doughnut shop, rest in the parked car," Stanwick said as Walker's face began to redden. "Well, you say it's been a long week. Any particular case on your mind?"

"Only extortion and murder," replied Walker, still irritated. "The Harland Avenue syndicate runs an extortion operation in that end of town. Many of the small shops there pay 'protection' money. Our racketeering unit's been after them for months.

"Now there's been a homicide," he continued more calmly. "Josie Welch owned Welch Electronics, a small computer repair shop on Harland. She refused to pay up, and last week the gang decided to make an example of her."

"How was it done?" Stanwick asked somberly.

"Four members of the syndicate visited the shop about five last Friday afternoon," said Walker. "While one waited in the car, three of them, including the driver, went inside. Some shouting was heard, and then one of them beat Welch to death with a small club that was left at the scene. No fingerprints. The killer was neither the driver nor the one who set the shop on fire just before they all fled in the car."

"How much fire damage was done?"

"Not too much. Someone in a shop across the street saw the smoke and called it in. Our investigators are cooperating with the RFD arson squad."

Stanwick toyed with the tip of his mustache.

"Since you know the four were members of the syndicate," he said, "I presume you have an idea who they were."

"You are correct, sir," replied Walker with a grim smile. "This was an equal-opportunity assault: two men and two women. They were John Mears, Edie Sullivan, Debra Hassey, and George Higgins. The arsonist, the killer, a backup thug or lookout, and a driver, in some order. We're still gathering information from witnesses, snitches, and other sources."

"I suppose these four have priors," Stanwick remarked.

"Yes, but our information is incomplete. Many files were lost in another fire—the big one at the archives repository several years back. We do know that all four did time in Chisholm Penitentiary. One did three years, another did six, and the others did nine and twelve years. While there, they had amusing little 'pastimes.' One tried digging an escape tunnel—right into the warden's office. Another boned up on legal aid and appeal procedures. A third ran drugs. The fourth specialized in enforcing the pen's unwritten 'rules.' We just don't know which was which!"

"Ah yes, that unfortunate fire!" Stanwick laughed. "It's caused many a head-scratch. I hope your other info sources are reliable."

"I think so. Word of the murder and the fire got on the street quickly—as I'm sure the syndicate intended by making an example of Welch. Would you like to know what we have so far?"

"By all means."

Walker extracted a small notebook from his pocket and flipped over several pages.

"The legal aid expert was in prison for nine years," he said, "which was half again as long as the arsonist. The backup thug is either Mears or Higgins. Neither the arsonist nor Hassey was either the drug runner or the tunnel digger while in prison."

"You'll give me a headache yet," remarked Stanwick. "Do you have anything more specific?"

"Yes, a bit," replied Walker. "Sullivan was the prison 'enforcer.' Mears, who is not the backup thug, was in prison only half as long as Sullivan. The driver has never known a thing about legal aid, and the drug-runner was not the one who served the longest prison term."

Stanwick smiled as he jotted notes on the back of a chess scoresheet.

"Go home and sleep on it, napless one," he said as he handed the scoresheet over to Walker. "With a clearer brain, you should be able to verify these deductions. Here are the identities of your killer and the rest!"

Who is the killer?

Solution on page 88.

The Case of the Forged Will

THOMAS P. STANWICK could not help marveling at the contrast between the offices of his two closest police friends, Inspector Matthew Walker of the Royston Police and Inspector Gilbert Bodwin of Scotland Yard. Walker's office was chronically cluttered, but Bodwin kept his scrupulously tidy. Just a matter of working style, Stanwick concluded as he looked around Bodwin's office once more.

"I'll be in London for ten days," Stanwick remarked to Bodwin, who was seated behind his desk. "See the old sights, hit the theaters and the bookshops. Then to Cambridge for a few days, then to the East Anglia countryside to see the Earl, and finally to Edinburgh for a logic conference."

"Sounds appalling," said Bodwin with a wry smile. "What gets discussed at a logic conference?"

"The topic this year is the assumption of existential import and

its effect on Aristotle's traditional square of opposition. Riveting stuff, I assure you. So—anything exciting at the Yard these days?"

"Nothing to match Aristotle. A man died last month and turned out to have a forged will."

"A will, eh?" Stanwick leaned back and cupped his hands behind his head. "Is there much money involved?"

"There is, actually. Several millions. Freddie Teti made a pile as a software entrepreneur and popped off recently at fifty-two with a chronic blood disease."

"Doesn't sound like a murder, anyway."

"No. Teti's solicitor, William Chellman, became suspicious of the will when he found that it left Teti's estate to three relatives. Chellman tells us that he had drawn up a will for Teti several years earlier that left his entire fortune to a medical foundation. Teti had kept the will on file at his home and not left Chellman a copy.

"Shortly before his death," Bodwin continued, "Teti said to Chellman that the bequest to the foundation might be the best, as well as the last, thing he ever did. Yet when Chellman found the will in Teti's home files, it left everything equally to a cousin, a niece, and a nephew. Chellman says he is sure that Teti would have had him draw up any revised will. So he called us in."

"Has your lab examined the will?" asked Stanwick.

"Yes. The critical pages are of newer paper than the rest, when a revised will would normally have been entirely reprinted. Also, our handwriting people believe that the signatures on the last page are forged."

"I see. And who are the surprise—and possibly surprised—beneficiaries?"

"Teti's cousin is Arthur Dietzel, a major in the American army," said Bodwin. "Teti's aunt married a Yank, you see. He's 48, and was stationed in London last year at the American Embassy. The nephew, John Manning, is also an American. Teti's sister carried on the family tradition of marrying across the pond. He's 25, and is working on a doctoral thesis in geology."

"And the niece?"

"Barbara Teti is British, oddly enough. Daughter of Teti's brother, age 27, and a commercial pilot."

"Perhaps she then had the most opportunities to visit her uncle," Stanwick remarked.

"Perhaps, but we know that the major visited Teti in March of '01, just fourteen months ago, and that Manning spent a week with his uncle in September. All three of them spent a few days with Teti at Christmastime."

"May I see the will?"

"If you like. The lab is done with it. It's there on the table."

Stanwick strode to a side table and carefully turned over the pages of the will.

"Hmm." Stanwick peered closely at the last page. "I see it was signed 'of my own free will this 11th day of February, 2001' purportedly by Teti and then two witnesses whose scribbles I can't read. The forgery would have occurred on or after the given date, of course. And all three beneficiaries were known to have stayed with Teti between that date and Teti's death."

"Precisely."

A crisp knock on Bodwin's door was followed by the entry of a sergeant bearing a slip of paper.

"Thought you should see this, sir," the sergeant said to Bodwin. "I had another look in Mr. Teti's file cabinet, and found this in the bottom of the folder where the will had been kept."

"Thank you, Fogg," said Bodwin. "Let's see. Handwritten in blue ink on white paper. 'Will revised 2/11/01. Sole copy. F. T.' Well! That would seem to eliminate one of our suspects."

"Even better." Stanwick smiled. "I think it eliminates two."

What suspect was left, and why?

Solution on page 89.

The Fainting Trader

"I HAVE BEEN ROBBED!" shouted the caller to Royston Police headquarters just after eight one morning.

"What's your name, sir? Where are you?" asked the operator.

"Jean-Luc Montbleu. 1287 Thornton Avenue, Suite 205. Hurry!" *Click.* Despite the caller's French accent, the operator noted the address correctly and notified Inspector Matt Walker. The amateur logician, Thomas P. Stanwick, happened to be in the inspector's office just then. Responding to the call, they entered the offices of MMCH Traders at quarter past eight.

The two men found Montbleu at his desk in an inner office, head in hands. When they entered, Montbleu looked up and swept his arm toward his wall cabinets.

"Gone!" he cried. "It was here last night, but this morning— *pfft!*" Then he fainted, his head falling back against his chair.

"Call the EMT's, Tom," growled Walker. Stanwick grabbed the desk phone.

"Sir, can you hear me?" Walker shouted. "What was stolen?"

Montbleu's eyes fluttered, and he murmured something before

fainting again. Walker swore.

"Medics are on the way," said Stanwick, hanging up. "What did he say was stolen?"

"He didn't," Walker replied grimly. "All he said was 'enough'. Enough what?"

"Let's look around," said Stanwick. "I've heard of this firm. Four partners sell exotic items wholesale. Most are stored elsewhere, but they keep samples here, as well as some of their personal collections. This office, as you can see, has gold-headed canes, antique dolls, jeweled eggs, diamond cufflinks, silver medallions, and ruby rings. The cufflinks and rings are in labeled boxes, and the rest are loose on the counters. Pretty poor security."

Walker went to the outer office and then returned.

"Just a table and file cabinets there," he said. "The other inner offices are locked. Let's wait for the medics and the other partners to show up."

At eight-thirty, after Montbleu had been taken away, Roy Monroe arrived. Walker told him what had happened, showed him Montbleu's office, and then questioned him in his.

"I don't know what was taken, detectives," he said. "Jean-Luc is the senior partner, and only he keeps track of his inventory. The written records are in poor shape, I'm afraid."

"Anything missing in here?" asked Stanwick.

"Don't think so." Monroe counted several sealed boxes on his floor and checked the old books, jeweled eggs, and cufflink sets in glass cabinets on his wall. "My share of inventory is here, as well as my own collection."

"Mr. Montbleu implied that the theft occurred last night," said Walker. "Can you tell me where you were?"

"I got an early supper at my neighborhood café, and then watched an old war movie in my apartment before turning in. Alone."

Margaret Houston arrived at nine. Told of the incident, she peered around Montbleu's office through thick glasses. Her office also had several sealed boxes, but her glass cabinets displayed rare dolls and sets of ruby rings.

"No one but Jean-Luc could tell if something was missing from his office, Inspector," she said. "His set of canes looked a little thin, maybe. Nothing seems to be missing in here. Last night? I went for a late afternoon bike ride, then went home for spaghetti. I live alone—divorced. From eight to nine I talked with my mother on the phone. Then I arranged some of my doll collection and went to bed."

Oscar Cantini arrived at quarter past nine. He too was informed of the incident, shown Montbleu's office, and questioned. Besides the sealed boxes on the floor, his office included a cluster of gold-headed canes and displays of silver medallions. He shook his head.

"No, I couldn't tell you what was taken from Jean-Luc's office," he said. "Roy and Margie will tell you that only he kept inventory of his stuff. All my things are here, though."

"Where were you last night?" Walker smiled.

"I saw a film at the cinema and got some drive-through Chinese for supper. Ate it at home, then went to bed. No, I didn't see anyone I knew at the cinema."

A few hours later, Stanwick and Walker were eating burgers at a diner downtown. Stanwick had just returned from the phone.

"Montbleu is in a coma," he said. "He has relatives near Paris, who are being notified."

"Great!" exclaimed Walker with disgust. "So we still don't know what was stolen."

"True, but at least we know the thief was probably one of the partners. There were no signs of forced entry, and the same key works for all the inner offices. And they were collectors, so they might have stolen to add to their collections at home rather than to sell."

"I agree. And we saw what each one collects. Which makes it all the more frustrating not to know what was taken!" Walker chewed angrily at his burger.

Stanwick paused, water glass in hand, and slowly smiled.

"Wait a minute, Matt," he said. "I think I know what was stolen. And who our prime suspect is!"

Who was Stanwick's prime suspect, and why?

Solution on page 89.

Stanwick and the Living Lawnmower

THE COUNTRY AIR felt crisp and cool that Tuesday afternoon in early September. Thomas P. Stanwick and his black Labrador, Rufus, were enjoying a long ramble in the farm country just outside Baskerville. Stanwick had spent the morning studying Civil War letters in the archives of the Baskerville Historical Society, to research an essay he was contributing to a book on local history. Though he found the letters fascinating, he was quite ready afterward for a hike in the open.

As he and Rufus approached George Green's farm, Stanwick saw a Baskerville neighbor, Jerry Bredon, talking intently with farmer Green near the road. Stanwick, who knew both men, approached and greeted them.

"Why hello, Tom," said Green. "Jerry here is trying to rent a living lawnmower."

"Beg your pardon?" Stanwick smiled.

"It's very simple, Tom," Bredon said, a thin vein showing on his forehead. "Very simple. One of my tavern buddies, Bob, has bet me that farm animals are no good for trimming lawns, and are only good for grazing in open fields. I know otherwise. George here has a bull, a mule, and a sheep that he's willing to rent to me individually or in any combination, starting tomorrow morning.

"The sheep doing it alone would take four days to chomp my yard, but my Martha insists that the job be done before her parents arrive at five on Thursday afternoon. Bob can't stop by until Thursday noon, though, and I need him to see the work in progress to convince him and win my bet."

Stanwick laughed heartily.

"That's cutting it rather fine!" he exclaimed. "Pun intended. Can your fine animals measure up, George?"

"They can," drawled Green. "My bull trims an acre a day. My sheep trims half an acre a day, and my mule does half an acre every couple of days. I've used them for yard work myself sometimes."

Stanwick whistled to Rufus, who was starting to wander down the road.

"Would you have the animal or animals you rent start and stop at the same time every day until the job was done, Jerry?" he asked as Rufus trotted back.

"You bet. George here is very particular about what a rental 'day' is. Seven to five."

Stanwick idly twisted an end of his droopy mustache and then smiled.

"In that case," he said, "I think I can tell you what you should rent to get your lawn trimmed between Thursday noon and Thursday evening, thereby winning your wager and preserving your marriage."

"Wait a minute, Tom!" Bredon exclaimed. "I haven't even told you how big my yard is!"

Stanwick chuckled. "Yes, you have."

What should Bredon rent?

Solution on page 89.

The Adventure of the Speckled Strap

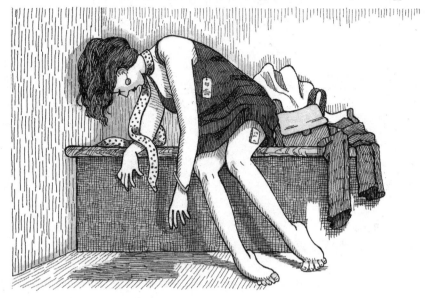

A SCREAM FROM the third floor of Schweppe's department store prompted Stanwick and Inspector Walker to drop their cheeseburgers at the lunch counter and rush up the escalator.

Most of the third floor was covered with racks of women's clothing, especially the pants for which Schweppe's was famous. In the center of the floor was a hut of fitting rooms, with doors facing the escalator and full-length mirrors on the sides. A store clerk was staring into one of the open fitting rooms, frozen but no longer screaming.

Sitting crumpled on the fitting room bench was the body of a woman in her late forties. She was of average height and build, and her made-up complexion was as artificial as the red tint of her hair. A price tag hung from the plain black dress she wore. Beside her on the bench were a blue blouse, matching pants, and a handbag. The most riveting apparel item in the tiny room, however, was the speckled strap bound tightly around the woman's neck.

The inspector examined the handbag and identified the victim as Ethel May Clarke. He then called in the crime-scene unit and

briefly questioned the store clerk who had discovered the body. A few hours later, after visiting Clarke's mother, he and Stanwick were in Walker's car heading for an interview with one of Clarke's friends.

"For a woman who took such trouble over her looks," Walker remarked, "Clarke had a remarkably small social circle. Her mother spoke with her every day but could name only two friends. Father dead. No husband or siblings."

"It's especially surprising," agreed Stanwick, "since her work as a freelance photographer undoubtedly brought her in contact with a wide range of people. On the other hand, the work probably required much travel, which can disrupt one's personal life. I think this is Glynn's address."

Velma Glynn was the same age as Ethel Clarke. Her short hair was naturally brunette, however, with a streak of gray. She answered her door cautiously.

"Ms. Glynn, I'm Inspector Walker of the Royston Police," said Walker, showing his badge. "This is Mr. Stanwick. I'm sorry to tell you a friend of yours, Ethel Clarke, was strangled in a fitting room at Schweppe's department store earlier today. Her mother gave us your name, and we were hoping you could tell us about her recent activities and acquaintances."

"Ethel murdered! My Lordie." Glynn numbly waved them into her living room, where they all sat down. "I—I can't imagine who could have harmed her, Inspector. Of course, she had to do some traveling for her photography, so she may have met someone she didn't tell me about."

"When did you last talk with her?" asked Stanwick.

"About five days ago, on the phone. I got back from a short trip myself only yesterday. Maybe she met someone since we talked. Did the strangler have big hands, a man's hands?"

"She was killed with a speckled strap, possibly a belt," replied Walker.

"Really! Was it from the dress she was trying on?"

"No, the dress was plain black."

Glynn smiled sadly and shook her head. "Poor Ethel always wanted to look chic."

"Had she expressed any worries to you recently?" asked Walker.

"No. A few weeks ago, though, she mentioned that she had seen a man she had dumped back in college staring at her in the mall. She smiled at him and he hurried away. She laughed it off."

"His name?"

"George. George…McGrath."

"Thank you. Pardon the routine question, but where were you today?"

"Quite all right." Glynn sighed deeply. "I'm an auto insurance adjuster. I was checking a few cases in Lakeview and got home just an hour ago. Here's my travel log."

"Thank you, Ms. Glynn. Here's my card. Please call if any other incident occurs to you, no matter how trivial."

Once they were back in the car, Stanwick turned to Walker.

"I'll be interested to hear what Friend #2 has to say about Velma," he said. "She should be investigated further."

"She will be, of course. That's routine. But why do you say that?"

"Because, my friend, Velma knows much more about the murder than she told us just now."

Why does Stanwick suspect Velma Glynn?

Solution on page 90.

The Frequent Flier from Rio

"A NACONDA SKINS!" Thomas P. Stanwick stared blankly at his plate of veal and eggplant parmigiana.

"It's an unusual smuggling case, yes," replied FBI special agent Ryan Cooper across the table from him. "Some Asian immigrants grind the skins up and use them as medicine. They're very valuable."

"Not to mention very illegal," added Inspector Walker. The three of them were having dinner at the Casa Italia in Royston.

"Jaime Gandolfo is a Brazilian suspected by the Rio police of smuggling anaconda skins into the U.S.," Cooper said. "He uses the fortnightly Amazonian Air nonstop flight from Rio to Royston. That's how Customs, the FBI, and Royston's finest got involved."

"And together you want to put the squeeze on Gandolfo," remarked Stanwick dryly.

"You could put it that way—although I wish you wouldn't." Cooper grimaced.

"Each time Gandolfo arrives here," he continued, "Customs thoroughly—and I mean thoroughly—examines him, his briefcase, and his suitcase, but never finds anything incriminating to deny him entry. Lately the other passengers have been getting the same treatment, just in case. Gandolfo checks into the Palisade Hotel, insisting on the same room every time, and stays for three days. Within a day of his arrival, we get word through our contacts here that skins are being sold in Asian immigrant neighborhoods."

"Has he been tailed?" asked Stanwick.

"Of course. He always slips away for a time, though, and has never been caught making the sale. There's no doubt he's moving the skins. It's just a matter of finding out how and catching him."

"He would have to get the skins onto the plane somehow." Stanwick carefully twirled his linguini. "Is he searched at the Rio end before boarding?"

"Only perfunctorily," frowned Cooper. "The Rio police think he bribes airport security there."

"How large would the package of skins have to be?" asked Walker.

"Only about the size of a large book. A little anaconda skin goes a long way."

"Sounds like a slimy but enterprising fellow," said Stanwick. "Does he treat himself to first class?"

"No, he flies coach. He's very fat, though, so he buys all three seats on a side row to accommodate himself."

"Is he really fat," Walker asked, grinning, "or might he have a package under his shirt?"

"No chance. As I said, Customs is thorough."

"Perhaps he has an accomplice on the flight crew," suggested Stanwick.

"Nice try, but the crew is changed for every flight. Besides, they have to pass through Customs too. The Rio police have watched several crew members on the off chance but have seen nothing suspicious."

Walker leaned back and scratched his chin.

"These flights," he said. "Do they go on from here?"

"No," replied Cooper. "The plane stays here overnight and then returns to Rio the next day. The airport authority keeps it under tight overnight security. So how do we get Gandolfo? So far we have nothing."

"Instead of nothing, we have the answer," said Stanwick. He smiled over a forkful of eggplant. "I can suggest how Gandolfo is smuggling the skins off the plane. Knowing that should enable you to unravel the whole setup."

How is Gandolfo smuggling the skins?

Solution on page 90.

Death of a Rye Writer

A DOORBELL PRESSED by Inspector Walker interrupted Stanwick's afternoon nap.

"I'm on my way to Rye," Walker explained when Stanwick groggily answered the door. "Gerald McCourt, the writer, has been murdered. The Rye police chief requested assistance from the Royston PD. Come along if you'd like."

"There hasn't been a murder in Rye in years," remarked Stanwick as he entered Walker's car. "Sorry to be so bleary. Today's the 23rd, right? I was up most of the night studying some downloaded manuscript notes of Jacques Futrelle, the mystery writer who created The Thinking Machine and went down with the Titanic."

"This case should interest a literary type like you," said Walker sardonically. "You've heard of McCourt?"

"Oh, yes. A prolific novelist, and very reclusive. Hasn't appeared in public in many years, though he grants occasional profile interviews. He's very compulsive in his habits. When drafting a manuscript, he works from eight A.M. until noon and from ten to two at night, every day but Sunday, banging out two pages an hour on a manual typewriter."

"Not a computer?" Walker arched his sandy eyebrows.

Stanwick shook his head. "He's—was—in his mid-seventies, and never changed his methods."

McCourt's body was being removed from his study when Walker and Stanwick arrived. Sunlight streamed through the only window onto the book-lined walls. Several dusty books were on the cluttered typing table. Page 250 was still in the typewriter, and a pile of manuscript lay beside it.

"McCourt was sitting at his typewriter," Sergeant Hatch reported to Walker. "Doc Pillsbury found a hypodermic puncture mark on the back of his neck. He says it was definitely poison, but won't know which until after the autopsy and a toxicology test."

"Time of death?" asked Walker.

"Doc can't tell yet," replied Hatch. "Some poisons affect the deterioration of the body. It could have been last night or this morning. The housekeeper phoned in at eleven this morning. She, McCourt, and McCourt's daughter are the only ones to have been in the house recently. The house is kept locked up tight, and the locks show no sign of tampering."

"Where are the housekeeper and the daughter now?"

"In the kitchen, sir."

At the kitchen table Walker and Stanwick found Ann McCourt Kitchens and Hildegard Conti. Kitchens, the writer's daughter, was in her mid-thirties, tall and thin, with long brown hair. The housekeeper, Conti, was in her early sixties. She wore her graying hair in a bun over a wrinkled, freckled face.

"I work in New York as a playwright, Inspector," said Kitchens. "I've been visiting Daddy for almost two weeks. I last saw him at ten this morning, when I looked in on him in his study to say hi and tell him I was going into town. I met an old friend of mine, Mary Anderson, at the Home Plate diner for a late breakfast. We were there until about noon. When I returned, the police were here."

"I understand you found Mr. McCourt, Ms. Conti," said Walker.

"Yes, sir," Conti replied. "I had breakfast in here as usual and then cleaned up the dishes and dusted the living room. Mr. McCourt doesn't eat breakfast, so I don't see him until I bring him tea in the

study at eleven. When I did today, I found him slumped at the typewriter. I screamed, dropped the tea tray, and phoned 911."

"Did you hear Mr. McCourt typing earlier?" asked Stanwick.

"I never do, sir. He types quietly and keeps the door closed, and my hearing is only so-so."

"Did you see Ms. Kitchens leave this morning?" asked Walker.

"Yes, sir, a little after ten."

Walker thanked them, and he and Stanwick returned to the study.

"They spoke to Hatch earlier," said Walker, "and he's made some inquiries. The housekeeper has been here over twenty years. The daughter did arrive a couple of weeks ago for a visit. She's divorced. McCourt had been working on a new manuscript since Monday the 5th, so he might have been working in the study both last night and this morning. Mary Anderson confirms her late breakfast with the daughter."

"You're right, Matt, it's an interesting case," said Stanwick. He smiled. "There's a particularly logical twist to it. If you'd like, I can tell you when McCourt was murdered and point out the murderer right now."

Who murdered Gerald McCourt?

Solution on page 91.

Theft in a Knordwyn Shop

ENGLAND WAS ONE of Thomas P. Stanwick's favorite summer destinations. Among the amateur logician's regular haunts was the beautiful Northumbrian village of Knordwyn. Its cobbled streets, crooked streams, and surrounding green hills were particularly soothing to his eye, and the peculiarities of its inhabitants were particularly intriguing to his mind. Half of them never told the truth, and the other half never lied. His powers of deduction were therefore often tested.

One day in late August, Stanwick arrived in Knordwyn, checked into the Grey Boar Inn, and took a long late-morning walk through the village. After lunching at a pub near the village square, he walked down a nearby street and knocked on the door of an old friend, truthteller Winston Langworth, who was the chief constable in Knordwyn.

"Thomas!" boomed Langworth when he answered the door. His large, ruddy face, framed by a Lincoln beard, showed his surprise. "I wasn't expecting you, but do come in. We thought you would be here for the Queen Anne Festival, which ended ten days ago."

"Sorry I couldn't attend the festival this year," said Stanwick as he was ushered to the front parlor of Langworth's small home. "I had an editing project to finish up back home."

"Pity. There was an especially good juggling troupe this year. Ah, well, you're just in time."

"In time for what?"

"To help me unravel a little robbery case."

"Oh?" Stanwick eased himself into an armchair and lit his pipe. "Who's been robbed?"

"David Ashton, the dispensing chemist up on High Way. A bag of cash receipts was taken from behind the counter of his shop this morning."

"Hmm." Stanwick reminded himself that a dispensing chemist in Britain was the same as a pharmacist in the States. He also suppressed the impulse to make a bad pun about High Way robbery. "Behind the counter. Is his clerk suspected?"

"No. Like Ashton, Marianne Witherby is a truthteller, and she denies stealing it. When I visited the shop, I saw that anyone could have reached under the cash register, where the bundle had been kept, and taken it. Marianne says the bag was there at nine this morning when she added some notes to it for a later bank deposit.

"The only entrance to the shop is the front door," continued Langworth, "and a bell rings whenever the door opens. Only three people visited the shop this morning, all at different times. Any of them might have gotten near the counter while Marianne was busy elsewhere. When she returned to the counter at noon to prepare the deposit, the bag was gone. No customers were there at the time, but she raised the alarm with Ashton, who was in the back room having tea."

Stanwick gratefully accepted a cup of Earl Grey. "Was Marianne able to identify that morning's three customers?"

"She was. All three are villagers, but we don't know whether they are liars or truthtellers. I called them and asked them to come by here for a chat."

The first arrived a few minutes later. Jane Speakman, a barmaid in her late twenties, sported a black jacket, a black skirt, and black boots. Her blue eyes helped set off a small nose ring. She was followed shortly by Joseph Sweeney, a garage mechanic in his thirties. His red beard was framed by a cap and grease-stained overalls. Langworth's final visitor was Robert Snow, a clean-shaven solicitor in his early forties who wore a three-piece suit. He nervously ran his hand through his thinning sandy hair as the five of them sat down in the parlor.

"Thank you all for coming," said Langworth blandly. "I told each of you on the phone of the theft at the chemist's this morning. You three were the only visitors during that time, and I have reason to believe that the clerk is innocent. One of you must therefore be the thief. And perhaps those who are not know who is."

"I've never stolen anything in my life," said the barmaid emphatically. "The three of us hardly know each other, in any case."

"She's right," added Sweeney. "I certainly didn't steal the money."

"In fact, we three know each other rather well," said the solicitor. "Either I did not steal the money or Sweeney here is innocent."

Langworth frowned and cleared his throat. "I can assure you that I will get to the bottom of this matter."

"Indeed, constable, you already have," remarked Stanwick languidly, with only a hint of gentle sarcasm in his tone. "Congratulations on a brilliant interrogation. The identity of the thief is quite clear."

Who stole the money from the shop?

Solution on page 91.

The Talk of the Pub

A SCORE OF Knordwyn villagers and one out-of-town visitor crowded the pub of the Grey Boar Inn that warm August evening. The tang of smoke, the clink of mugs, the thunk of darts on a board, and the hum of voices were soothing to the visitor, Thomas P. Stanwick, who was happily weary from a day-long hike in the surrounding hills.

Stanwick shared a table with Philip Mangone. The amateur logician did not know whether Mangone was one of the villagers who always told the truth, or instead one who always lied. Nor did he know that about a nearby villager wearing a checked cap. The others there, he knew, were consistent truthtellers.

The main topic of conversation in the pub that evening was the recent death of a local squire.

"There never was a more honest and truthful man than Hugh Cronin," declared John "Doc" Kelly.

"That's right," responded Bill Manooshian. "When the will is read next week, we'll see where he left his money. He told me not long ago that he would leave it all either to Henry Kinsley, who runs the Homeless Veterans Fund, or to Ruth Segal, who runs the Disabled Children's Trust."

"Harry Kinsley! There's an odd duck." Phyllis Glynn laughed. "Badly allergic to wool and feathers, he is, but he still owns a small sheep farm. Won't go near any creature that sets off his allergies, though. Ruthie is a dear. She lives for those children."

"At least Cronin didn't require all his visitors to pat his pets on the head," remarked Mangone. "My mum still does."

"Did the squire have many pets?" asked Stanwick.

"Five turtles, three snakes, a llama, and an iguana," said Marie Doucet. "My youngest used to sit for his kids. The Cronins have always loved exotic creatures."

"I had a good talk with the squire last year," remarked Bob Cormier, the villager with the checked cap. "He said he would never leave a penny to anyone who would not visit him at home. Hardly a problem, I imagine. His sherry was always very good."

Mangone leaned over to Stanwick.

"Don't pay no attention to Bob," he whispered. "He's a liar. He even admits it."

Stanwick smiled and took a sip of ale.

"So the will is being read next week," he mused aloud. "Well, it's clear enough who will be pleased by its terms."

Who will inherit the squire's money?

Solution on page 92.

The Case of the Kidnapped Consultant

OCTOBER, ESPECIALLY WHEN rainy, was not Stanwick's favorite month to visit London. The chance to watch a world championship chess match, however, was enough to lure him across the sea. At eight o'clock on his first morning there, he called on Gilbert Bodwin at the inspector's office in New Scotland Yard.

"Glad to see you, Tom," said Bodwin as he pawed through some papers on his desk. "Have to go out on a case in a moment, though. Welcome to come if you like."

"Delighted." Stanwick grinned at the laconic diction Bodwin adopted when in a hurry. "What case?"

"Beatrice Russell received a call at quarter to twelve last night saying her husband had been kidnapped. Two million ransom." Bodwin paused briefly to peruse a sheet of paper. "Samuel Russell is managing director of Liquidity Solutions Limited, a small financial consulting company. Usually works noon to midnight at the company suite in an office block near the City. Detectives saw Mrs. Russell at home and then went to the suite, where his office showed signs of a hasty departure."

"Does the building have a guard?" asked Stanwick.

"Yes, in the lobby. The night guard saw no one enter or leave after Russell's secretary left at seven-thirty. The only other access to the suite is by an elevator from the underground garage. The security computer confirms that the garage was accessed by code shortly after ten. Russell's car is missing from the garage, so we think the kidnappers used his own car to take him away. Ah, here's my folder. Let's be off."

"Did the day guard notice anything unusual yesterday?" Stanwick asked as Bodwin drove them toward the City section of London.

"No. He heard the garage elevator several times throughout the day. The night guard heard it about quarter past ten last night and again ten minutes later. He can never tell from the sound whether the elevator is ascending or descending."

"Do all Liquidity employees use the garage?"

"No, just Russell. Employees of other companies in the building use it too, of course. The other Liquidity employees did until a few months ago, when some nearby construction tied up traffic so badly that they switched to using the tube. Russell's odd hours made traffic less of a problem for him."

Stanwick and Bodwin were soon in the Liquidity Solutions office suite. The two paused at Russell's office and observed signs of a sudden exodus: cold coffee, dropped papers, computer and lights left on. They then went to a nearby conference room, where detectives had sent the three other Liquidity employees as they arrived for work.

"I'm Inspector Bodwin of the Yard," the inspector announced. "Mr. Russell was abducted from his office last evening. His abductor or abductors apparently came and went by means of the garage elevator. I would like to hear from each of you whether Mr. Russell had been receiving threats or seemed nervous or excited. Please also tell me when you saw him last and where you were last evening."

"I know of no threats, sir," said a black woman in her early thirties. She wore a dark blue jacket, a matching skirt, and a white blouse. "I'm Tanisha Kvicala, Mr. Russell's secretary. He seemed fine. I was here with him until seven-thirty, as usual, and then went home by tube after picking up some Chinese takeaway."

"Were you then home all evening?" asked Bodwin.

"Yes. Poor Beatrice! How much ransom is being demanded?"

"Sorry, can't discuss that. And you, sir?" Bodwin addressed himself to a tall, lanky man in his fifties wearing a new gray suit. He had short straw-yellow hair, and a pair of steel-rimmed glasses were perched atop a long, red-tipped nose.

"I'm Harding, Inspector," the man said. "Lawrence Harding. Vice president of investment services for the last four years. I know of no threats, and saw nothing unusual in Sam's demeanor. I left at six, my usual time, and went to the theater with my wife. That Shakespeare thingy at the New Globe. Tell me, have you recovered Sam's car yet? I understand they often have clues and such."

"Not yet, sir." Bodwin turned to the third employee, a woman in her forties with long, black hair and heavy makeup. She blinked in a way that suggested either tears or faulty contact lenses.

"My name is Eva Kantor," she said quietly. "Vice president for client outreach. I saw nothing unusual either. I left a little after six, leaving only Samuel and Tanisha still here, and went straight home to my husband and son. Jerry always has supper waiting."

"Thank you. Please wait here." Bodwin signaled to Stanwick and left the room with him. They found a small kitchenette down the hall, and Bodwin began to prepare a kettle for tea.

"This case has some interesting features," remarked Stanwick as he sat down at a small table. "Have the garage access codes been changed recently?"

"Not in almost a year, the guards tell us," Bodwin replied.

"How about a trace on the ransom call?"

"We have a tap on the Russells' phone now, of course, but the original call cannot be traced."

"Well, that may not matter." Stanwick clasped his fingers behind his head. "At least you have one lead. One of those three is involved, and undoubtedly provided the access code to the kidnappers."

"There are a number of other companies in this office block whose employees use the garage," Bodwin pointed out.

"True. Nonetheless," Stanwick persisted, "one of those three is at least an accomplice. If you like, I can specify which one."

Which Liquidity employee does Stanwick suspect?

Solution on page 92.

A Shocking Christmas

IT WAS TWO days before Christmas, and a cold snap following a snowfall was keeping the sidewalks of Royston icy. Stanwick braved them that afternoon and appeared in Walker's office at police headquarters with a bag of presents.

"An early Merry Christmas to you, Matt," he exclaimed cheerfully. Stanwick put the bag beside Walker's desk and sat down. "Just a few things for Elizabeth and the boys, and possibly yourself. I hope Peter and Tim still like board games."

"They do. Hey, this is nice of you, Tom. Thanks!" Walker leaned back in his chair. "Your present is, uh, in the mail, I'm told. So—will you be spending the holiday at your sister's?"

"Yup. I'm heading over there tomorrow with goodies for the lot of them. Any interesting holiday crimes on your plate?"

"Well, you may have heard of the death last night of Mary Turco, the interior decorating columnist."

"Heard it on the news." Stanwick thrust his hands in his pockets and stretched out his long legs. "Electrocuted in her own home, I understand. It sounded like an accident."

Walker shook his head. "Murder.

"She was showing off her Christmas decorations to some neighbors at a party at her home last night," he went on. "One of her fanciest exhibits was a big toy village on the dining room table. The village was lit and powered by lines and circuits under the table, all hidden by a large white tablecloth. Most of the circuits were set safely, but when she adjusted the village meeting house it gave her a shock that killed her. We found that the circuit to the meeting house had been deliberately tampered with."

"Hmm." Stanwick frowned. "Who had access to the circuitry?"

"Her husband Joe and teenage daughter Patricia live with her. Joe and one of the neighbors, Kathleen Carpenito, were with Mary at quarter past eight when she was electrocuted. Just before guests began arriving an hour earlier, Joe and Patricia saw Mary adjust all the village pieces harmlessly with the power on. She was compulsively neat, they tell us, and the neighbors agree. The killer may have moved the meeting house before altering the circuit, in order to provoke her to touch it. The only ones in the house that evening were Joe, Patricia, and three neighbors: Carpenito, Daniel Robertson, and Irene Brady."

"Were they definitely the only ones?" asked Stanwick. "How secure was the house?"

"Secure enough. The place has an alarm system and good locks, all undisturbed. We suspect the visiting neighbors rather than the husband and daughter."

"Why so?"

"Motive. There are no signs of domestic problems or any sort of affair. The victim carried very little life insurance, and the loss of her writing income is substantial. The neighbors, though, did have a motive."

"Indeed?" Stanwick raised an eyebrow, and his eyes glinted.

"They all live on a cul-de-sac, and a developer is offering these homeowners big bucks so that he can convert their places into condos. It's an all-or-nothing offer, though, and Mary Turco refused to sell. Her neighbors were furious at her. In fact, her husband says the party was partly an effort to make amends."

"Sounds like a good financial motive," agreed Stanwick. "The killer may have assumed that the husband would then be willing and maybe anxious to sell the house. I assume Hatch has been busy."

"I'd be lost without my bloodhound." Walker thumbed through a stack of papers on his desk and extracted two sheets of notes. "He's questioned everyone extensively. Robertson was the first to arrive at seven-fifteen, a quarter of an hour before the other two. Mary took him into the living room and showed him the decorations there. Joe and Patricia were in the recreation room, where Patricia remained until eight.

"When the other two arrived," Walker continued, "Joe took Brady into the living room for drinks while Carpenito joined Patricia in the rec room. Mary showed Robertson the dining room, where Joe and Brady heard them chatting for the next quarter of an hour. Robertson then joined Patricia in the rec room while Carpenito and Mary joined Joe in the living room."

"I suppose the Christmas tree was there, fully loaded," Stanwick said with a half-smile.

"Yes, it was," Walker replied, "and very impressively, too. Let's see....At eight, Brady returned to the living room and met Patricia there. Robertson, who had remained in the rec room, was joined by Mary for some pool, while Joe showed Carpenito the dining room display. Joe says neither of them touched the display. A quarter of an hour later, Brady and Patricia went to the rec room. Robertson returned to the living room for a drink, and Mary joined Joe and Carpenito in the dining room. That was when Mary starting adjusting the village display and got the shock of her life."

"Or her death," said Stanwick grimly. "Matt, are you sure that Joe and Patricia are being honest in their testimony?"

"Pretty sure. So far the circumstantial evidence has supported their statements."

"If we assume that, then I can suggest who your prime suspect is. Again, Merry Christmas!"

Who is Stanwick's prime suspect, and why?

Solution on page 92.

The Secret Scholarships

A<small>S USUAL FOR</small> a Wednesday, Baskerville's lone Italian restaurant was not crowded. Dining that evening in a quiet booth were Stanwick and his friend Amanda Tucker, an attorney.

"I haven't seen you in a while, Amanda," remarked Stanwick. "Anything or anyone special keeping you busy?"

"A case, unfortunately," Amanda replied with a smile. "A fellow named Lexner posed as a vacuum-cleaner salesman for highly dubious purposes, and my clients have filed a civil suit. We'll probably settle, though I have some entertaining witnesses lined up if it goes to trial. What have you been up to?"

"March is usually a busy month for me, and this is no exception. My major project was a special study of Latin word roots, which I just finished. I'm now editing a high school geometry text. Maybe Roger will be using it in a year or so."

"If so, he probably won't tell me," sighed Amanda. She was divorced, and her son was in high school. "He keeps everything to himself these days."

"That goes with his age," Stanwick reassured her. "It's not you."

"I know. But he's applying for a scholarship and won't even talk to me about that."

"A scholarship? He's only a sophomore, right?"

"Right, but he and his buddies Brian and Russ are applying for specialized scholarships that will help pay for college in a few years. Each scholarship requires a test in a particular field, one of which I know is chemistry. The mothers of the other boys are friends of mine, and we've talked on the phone about these scholarships, but none of us can tell what her son is applying for."

"Well, it doesn't sound like a conspiracy," said Stanwick with a grin. "Haven't the three of you found out anything at all about these scholarships?"

"Just snippets." Amanda sipped her wine while waiting for her antipasto salad. "Roger has mentioned that he's applying for the Ridgway, whichever one that is. Russ's mother says her son is applying for the history scholarship. And we've managed to find out that the math scholarship is not the Dickinson."

"How about Brian?"

"Brian's mom has found out that he is definitely not applying for the Tavorkian."

"Actually, you moms have done quite well," said Stanwick. "Of course, you could call the school to find out at least what subject each scholarship is in."

"Sure I could, but frankly I'm embarrassed to admit to them that my son won't talk to me." She stared softly at her wine.

Stanwick smiled and pulled out a small notebook.

"Well, if you'll allow me, I'll just jot down which lad is applying for which scholarship in what field," he said. "You and the other moms have already gathered enough pieces to put the puzzle together."

Can you match the students to the scholarships?

Solution on page 93.

Stanwick and the Stolen Bonds

BOB HARDING LOOKED worried as he opened his front door late one Saturday afternoon and let in Stanwick and Baskerville police chief William Ryan. Stanwick had been chatting with Ryan when Harding's call came in.

"Here in the basement," said Harding as the three descended the wooden steps. Harding, a lean, tall man with salt-and-pepper hair and a thin beard, was a retired automotive engineer. "I had $75,000 in bearer bonds in my safe yesterday, and now they're gone. The thief replaced the padlock, too. I had to saw it off."

Ryan peered closely at the small safe, now open, which rested on a steel shelf about six feet up and was bolted to the wall. It contained a passport and a clutter of papers. "You're sure the bonds were here yesterday?"

"Positive," Harding replied. "I'm thinking of taking a trip to France, and last night I checked my passport. The bonds were still here then. I'm a light sleeper and heard nothing during the nighttime, so I'm sure they were taken today."

"You were away, then," said Stanwick.

"Yes, at an estate auction in Littleton. Bought a letter signed by Charles Dawes, who was vice president under Coolidge. I got home about four-thirty and brought it down here for temporary safekeeping. When I couldn't work the padlock combination, I discovered that the lock wasn't mine, so I had to saw it. Only the bonds are missing."

The three men returned upstairs to the kitchen. Ryan excused himself for a few minutes to check the doors and windows.

"No forcible entry," he said when he returned. "Who has a key to this place?"

"Just me," replied Harding, "but I keep a spare under a flagstone in back."

"And who knew about the key and the bonds?"

"Only two friends of mine, Pat Greeley and Joe Fabiano, knew of both. One or the other usually waters my plant when I'm away. They also knew I would be away today. Our model car club met last Wednesday night, and I mentioned the auction."

"I didn't know you went to estate auctions, Bob," Stanwick remarked with a smile.

"It's a hobby, Tom. Usually I buy books, though, not documents."

"Did Greeley or Fabiano know the combination to your safe's padlock?" asked Ryan.

Harding shook his head. "Only I knew that. The thief must have sawn off the lock."

Ryan scratched the stubble on his chin. "I'll need to talk to your friends."

"Thought you would," said Harding as the doorbell rang. "Right after I called you, I called them, told them of the theft, and asked them to come over. Sounds like one of them is here now."

They both were. All five men were soon seated in Harding's living room. Greeley, a real estate agent, was slightly taller than Harding and had thin, sandy hair, bright freckles, and aviator glasses. Fabiano, a small man with tufts of hair around his ears, peered defiantly at Ryan through thick glasses. Ryan politely asked each where he had been that day.

"I was in Royston all morning," said Greeley. "At the Ganter-bridge Mall, getting a jump on my Christmas shopping. After lunch I showed two houses. Got home just before your call, Bob."

"I spent the morning doing chores," said Fabiano. "Taking the trash to the dump, buying groceries. Then I took my wife out for a long lunch at that new Malaysian place in Tewksbury."

"Do you have any idea who might have committed this theft?" asked Ryan.

Both men shook their heads. "Real shame about the bonds, Bob," Fabiano added.

"Thank you both," said Ryan as he stood up. "Be sure to let me know where you can be reached."

Two days later, Stanwick dropped by Ryan's office at headquarters. "Anything new on the Harding theft, Bill?"

"Well, we found footmarks between the woods and his house," said Ryan, leaning back and lacing his fingers behind his head. "Probably the thief's, but we couldn't determine the size. The key was under the flagstone, but not in its usual position, according to Harding. No fingerprints. The thief probably wore gloves."

"It's a pretty sparsely furnished place for someone who goes to estate auctions," remarked Stanwick. "Hardly anything in the basement but screens, shelves of model cars, and a furnace, and just books and big, clumsy furniture upstairs."

"Bob scaled back a lot after his wife died," said Ryan. "I verified that Greeley did conduct those house tours Saturday afternoon, and a supermarket clerk thinks he remembers seeing Fabiano in the store that morning. I haven't traced the replacement padlock yet, and frankly don't know why the thief bothered."

"He probably hoped to delay the discovery of the theft," Stanwick said. "He knew that Harding usually buys books at estate auctions, and could hardly have known that Harding had checked the safe just the night before. It was the thief's bad luck that Harding was able to pinpoint the day of the theft." Ryan nodded.

"Not bad investigating for a one-horse department, though," continued Stanwick with a grin. "You'll need to do some more before you can make an arrest, I think, but at least we know who the thief is."

Whom does Stanwick suspect as the thief?

Solution on page 93.

A Minivan Mystery

"SO—HAVE YOU found yourself a minivan yet?" asked Stanwick as he took off his coat and sat down.

"Still shopping," said Walker from across his desk. "It's a pain, but my family needs the space. Not like you singles."

It was a Tuesday morning in winter, and Stanwick had dropped by the inspector's office at police headquarters.

"A surprising number of singles get them too," remarked Stanwick.

"Actually, that's true," replied Walker. "I've discovered that in one of my current cases. That hit-and-run last Friday night."

"Oh? Tell me about it."

"It was about quarter of eleven." Walker leaned back in his chair. "A pharmacist named Susan Levine, age 27, left the skating rink on Harpwell Avenue and started to cross the street to get to her car in the opposite lot. According to our witness, a dark minivan that had been parked up the street, with its motor running but its lights off, suddenly peeled out and ran her down. Then it turned on its one working headlight and roared off."

"Who was this witness?" asked Stanwick.

"Fellow named Townley. An electrical engineer in his early sixties. He was walking to the rink to pick up his granddaughter. After the incident, he ducked into a convenience store to tell the clerk to call 911 and then went out to Levine. Nothing could be done."

"Could he describe the van?"

"Not in any detail, but he swears he got the license number: N68SXH. A genuine in-state plate, too, he says: the background color and glint were right. A streetlight was in just the right position. Trouble is, the Department of Motor Vehicles has no such number in its database."

Stanwick fingered the tip of his mustache. "Did the convenience store clerk see or hear anything?"

"Blind and deaf. At least where trouble was concerned. He did make the call, though. We found broken glass by the victim, apparently from one of the van headlights. We also found tire marks where the van peeled out from the sidewalk, but no brake marks."

"So it looks like deliberate murder."

"Exactly."

Stanwick shifted in his wooden chair. "Levine and the driver probably knew each other, then," he said.

"That's our working theory," said Walker. "And that's where the point about singles having minivans comes in. We checked the address book in Levine's apartment and found two people listed, both single, who happen to own dark blue vans that had body work done on them this past weekend."

"Really! That's remarkable. Quite a coincidence even if there had been no crime. Who are they?"

"One is Judy Magee, a research chemist and a college friend of Levine's. Works at Genotrom. Says she was watching TV in her apartment Friday evening. She tells us she has a minivan because she likes taking her sister's kids to events on Sundays when she can. According to her, she dented the van in a parking lot recently. Hatch talked to the sister, who says Magee hasn't taken the kids anywhere for three or four weeks."

"Maybe it's her busy season," said Stanwick.

"If chemists have them." Walker continued. "The other repaired van belongs to Michael Caponette, an assistant at an advertising agency. He claims to know Levine from high school, though we haven't confirmed that yet. Says he was seeing a movie alone at the Cineplex on Friday evening. His minivan, which he bought cheap from a cousin, slid on some ice last week and banged a post, he says."

"I suppose you have the good Sergeant Hatch out checking with the body shops," said Stanwick.

"And on a few other leads," Walker replied. "We have our eye on the pharmacy where Levine worked. It may be involved in a prescription drug ring."

Stanwick suddenly leaned forward, wrote on a pad of paper on Walker's desk, tore off the sheet, and handed it across.

"By any chance," he asked, "is this the license plate number of either of Levine's friends?"

Walker stared at the number and looked up at Stanwick in astonishment.

"Why, yes," he said. "This is Caponette's tag. Tom, how did you know that?"

"Just turning things over in my mind." Stanwick chuckled. "Caponette's your man."

How did Stanwick know the killer's real license plate number?

Solution on page 93.

The Impossible Poisoning

"NO, REGE, I don't deny the significance of assuming existential import," said Thomas P. Stanwick. "I just question whether existential import is implied in particular but not universal propositions."

"But consider the Venn diagrams!" exclaimed Regis Arnold, a philosophy professor at Royston State. "Those for universals are simply negations, but those for particulars posit the existence of a term."

"That may simply show the limits of the visual representation given by the diagrams," replied Stanwick with a smile. "Beware of visual literalism!"

The Shanghai Blossom restaurant in Royston was busy that spring evening. At one of its private tables, the Logic Club was holding its monthly dinner. Stanwick and Arnold were enjoying one of their occasional disputations about logical theory. Somewhat less engrossed in it were Inspector Walker, retired trial lawyer Whit Knowlton, attorney Amanda Tucker, and government statistician Susan Carlie.

"All right, enough of Aristotle *vs.* Venn for tonight!" said Tucker.

"Anyone have a toothsome puzzle?"

"Would you settle for an impossible crime?" answered Walker. "I'm investigating one right now."

"You can't be," said Knowlton. "If it happened, the crime must be possible."

"Well, seemingly impossible, then."

"Proceed, good inspector," said Carlie, smiling and raising her glass of wine.

"It concerns the death of one Frederick Mettler, the CFO of an Internet services company, at his office one morning last week," Walker began. "He collapsed within half an hour of consuming a cup of coffee."

"I've had office coffee like that," remarked Carlie.

"Finish your wine, Sue. The doc says Mettler ingested poison orally within the last few hours before his death. The trouble is, we don't see how it could have been the coffee.

"Mettler arrived at the office about quarter past seven," Walker continued. "An accountant and the office systems manager were already there. Bill Evans, the accountant, made the coffee as usual while chatting with Anibel Velasquez, the systems manager. They were still in the office kitchen when Mettler arrived, and all three drank from the same pot. The foam cups were from a newly opened pack. But Evans and Velasquez were unaffected."

"Did anyone have a chance to slip something into Mettler's cup after the coffee was poured?" asked Stanwick.

"No," replied Walker. "Mettler kept his cup in his hand until he returned to his office and drank it black, with no sugar. No one else had access to it."

"According to Evans and Velasquez," said Arnold. "Could they be lying?"

"They would have to be colluding," replied Walker. "There's no reason to believe that. They've only known each other a few months— Velasquez is new to the company—and what circumstantial evidence we've found supports their statements."

"So it wasn't the coffee," mused Arnold. "What are the alternatives?"

"None!" An edge of frustration entered Walker's voice. "Mettler was on a diet and had no coffee or breakfast at home. Not only did Mettler's wife tell us this: Mettler himself bragged about it to his office-mates that morning, and the autopsy showed no food in his stomach. We found no snacks in his office and no drive-through trash in his car. He took no medications. The aspirin in his house was unopened."

"Did he vary from his morning routine that day?" asked Knowlton.

"Apparently not," said Walker. "He and his wife, Sandy, have a small house on a quiet street. No kids. He washed up, shaved, showered, got dressed, and left for the office at seven. Sandy had tea and toast before leaving at eight for her job in a department store."

The group picked silently at Hunan chicken and spicy beef.

"Let's consider motive," said Carlie. "Has one come up?"

"Well, Evans is in line for Mettler's job," Walker replied. "Velasquez says there was also some office gossip about trouble in the Mettler marriage. She heard that Sandy wanted a separation but that Fred's religion prohibited it. The missus denies it, though. So, my logical friends: who murdered Fred Mettler, and how?"

"If we can answer the how, we'll know the who," said Carlie.

"Agreed," said Arnold, "unless, of course, it was suicide. Has that been ruled out?"

"For all practical purposes," said Walker. "There's no evidence of intent or motivation. And he didn't ingest that stuff accidentally. So it's murder, all right."

"It's also a nice disjunctive syllogism," said Stanwick. "Either A or B. Not A. Therefore B. You're saying you've eliminated all the alternatives, both A and B, which would make the crime truly impossible. As Whit points out, though, that itself is impossible. Therefore either A or B is still possible, or you've overlooked a C.

"I can construct at least one way in which the murder was committed," he continued, "and thereby tell you the identity of the murderer. Care to hear it?"

Who could have murdered Mettler, and how?

Solution on page 93.

A Carlie Conundrum

"WHAT'S MY FAVORITE government statistician working on nowadays?" asked Stanwick. He and Susan Carlie were having lunch in a downtown café one Monday in April.

"You remember that income tax cut that was passed a couple of years ago?" Carlie smiled and stirred her coffee. "Well, the economists in the revenue department were worried because it made total tax payments for the average family in the state dip below the cost of food, clothing, and shelter combined. So I was asked to do some research on the effects of the cut."

"And what were they?"

"Economic growth in the state is up, and so are private spending, saving, and investment. Some government economists, and even a few academic ones, are starting to believe that people who are allowed to keep and manage more of their own money can make sensible economic decisions for their families."

"Amazing!" Stanwick grinned. "You can now add 'instiller of wisdom' to your job description."

"Sure." Carlie snorted. "As if job descriptions mean anything."

"Why do you say that?"

"Well, job descriptions always have that little kicker at the end: 'Other duties as assigned.' Of course that means a job can include anything! And right now, mine includes a stint at editing the department newsletter, a chore for which my mathematical training hardly qualifies me."

"Oh, I'm sure you'll do fine. But how did that fall to you?" asked Stanwick.

"The editorship rotates around the department, and this month it's my turn." Carlie paused as a waiter laid soup and sandwiches on the table. "Here's my problem: everyone expects the newsletter to have details about vacations. This is school vacation week, so four of my colleagues are away. I thought descriptions of their vacations could wait until next month, when I wouldn't have to worry about it. This morning, though, my boss told me their vacation plans have to be in this month's newsletter!"

"So what's the problem?" Stanwick took a bite of a turkey club sandwich.

"The problem is that my deadline is in two days, and I have only sketchy details of their plans."

"Have you asked others in the office?"

"Yes, and I've gotten some information, but not enough."

"Maybe you could tell me what you have."

Carlie sighed and took a few sips of tomato soup.

"Helen, Bob, Charlie, and Joanie have each taken one child on vacation," she said. "The kids are two girls, Tanisha and Alison, and two boys, Andrew and Jimmy, who I remember is Bob's son. Their ages—and these are in no particular order—are 8, 10, 14, and one older but still a teenager. Alison is off to the Grand Canyon. Two others are vacationing at Disney sites, one (the 10-year-old) at Disneyland and the other at Disney World. The remaining parent and the 14-year-old child are at the Rock and Roll Hall of Fame in Cleveland."

"Cleveland!" Stanwick smiled. "I played in a chess tournament there once. Won a trophy. That was before the Hall of Fame, of course, back when Cleveland was the old Cleveland. What else have you learned?"

"Well, Joanie hates Disney, so she's not at either of those places," Carlie continued. "Her child, I understand, is twice as old as Charlie's. I heard at the water cooler that Helen has taken her son to one of the Disney sites."

Stanwick took out the pocket notebook and pen he always carried and jotted down some notes.

"I've always wanted to visit the Grand Canyon," he remarked, "but haven't gotten around to it yet. Maybe next year."

"Maybe. But can you give me a hand today, Tom? I think there's more to be deduced here, but I've been too busy to focus on it properly. If we were having a Logic Club meeting this week, I'd raise the problem there, but I'm up against my deadline."

"And you will meet your deadline with full particulars," said Stanwick as he finished writing and tore off two small sheets of paper. "You've gathered enough information to sort out who has taken whom of what age where!"

So who has taken which kid of what age where?

Solution on page 94.

Lunch at the Quill & Truncheon

Inspector Gilbert Bodwin of Scotland Yard and Thomas P. Stanwick silently entered the upstairs flat of Roger Sumner shortly before four one afternoon. Sumner, a tanned man in his fifties, was slumped back in a living room armchair, the fatal bullet wound just below his throat. His striped shirt and gray slacks, and the chair itself, were soaked in blood.

The small sofa pillow that had muffled the shot lay in foam ruins on the coffee table between Sumner's chair and the sofa. The other accoutrements of the room were unremarkable except for an oxygen tank propped in a corner. Police investigators quietly gathered fibers and other evidence.

Stanwick was in London at the start of a June vacation, and had been chatting with Bodwin at the Yard when the inspector was called to the Sumner flat.

Bodwin spoke briefly with two of the investigators. He and Stanwick then returned to the hallway at the beckon of Detective Sergeant Caulfield.

"This is Matthew Hanselman, sir," said Caulfield, nodding to a pale, dapper man beside him. "He found the body and phoned from a neighbor's flat downstairs."

"I sell insurance, inspector," Hanselman said nervously. "Disability insurance. I had a three o'clock appointment with Mr. Sumner. A parcel deliverer was going in just as I arrived, so I went in too and came up here to Mr. Sumner's flat, #3 like he said. When I got no answer to my knock, I tried the handle and found it unlatched. So I peeked in. There he was, all bloody and still. I ran downstairs in a panic, banged on the door of one of the flats, was let in, and called the police."

"Did you touch anything here before we arrived?" asked Bodwin.

"No, sir. I don't even like being here now!"

"Thank you, Mr. Hanselman. Please stand by." Bodwin turned to Stanwick. "Time for a chat with the neighbors. Care to come?"

"I would," replied Stanwick, "but I have dinner plans with some friends. How about lunch tomorrow at the Quill & Truncheon? You can catch me up."

The Quill & Truncheon was a small but popular pub between Fleet Street and the old Scotland Yard building, not far from the scene of the murder. The clink and hum of the luncheon crowd permeated its smoky confines as Stanwick and Walker settled themselves at a table shortly after noon the next day.

"I didn't mention yesterday," said Bodwin, "that Sumner, who made a legitimate living as a home-based advertising consultant, was also suspected of engaging in blackmail. We're still going through his papers, but that could be the motive behind his killing."

"It could," agreed Stanwick. "How did your talks with his neighbors go?"

"Well enough. The other upstairs flat is vacant. The two downstairs are occupied by elderly ladies. In Flat 1 lives Karen Sabre, a widow in her late seventies. She was looking out her window about eleven-thirty yesterday morning and saw Sumner return to the building. About a quarter past twelve, she saw another man, whom she didn't recognize, arrive and get buzzed in. Ruth Wentworth, who lives across the hall in Flat 2, also heard the buzz.

Miss Wentworth is a peppery spinster in her early eighties."

"Are she and Sabre friends?" asked Stanwick.

"Yes. In fact, about twelve-thirty Sabre joined her for lunch and some telly. They were still in Flat 2 shortly after three when Hanselman banged on the door and demanded to use the phone. Wentworth had already buzzed in the delivery fellow and received the parcel, some preserves from a cousin. She didn't see him or Hanselman come in, but she did see the delivery man leave."

"Did the neighbors know Sumner well?"

"They knew him slightly. He got out and about a good deal despite a gradually worsening asthma. You may have noticed that tank he kept handy."

Stanwick nodded and sipped his ale as he waited for his steak-and-kidney pudding. "I hope you had some luck tracing the mid-day visitor."

"Indeed. Constable McFarlane walks a beat in the area, and he recognized him from Sabre's description as one Paul Meyers, who runs an auditing firm nearby and often walks to lunch. When we caught up with Meyers in his office, he admitted that he had visited Sumner. He said Sumner had done some ad work for Meyers's firm, and they had remained friends.

"According to Meyers," Bodwin continued after lighting a small cigar, "he and Sumner were going to come here for lunch, as they did every month or so. Meyers stopped to collect Sumner, and they chatted briefly, but Sumner had forgotten about the appointment and said he had to do some work. So Meyers left and lunched alone."

"Of course, it would be helpful if you could confirm the delivery time of the Wentworth parcel," Stanwick remarked.

"We're working on that. Neither Wentworth nor Hanselman recall the delivery service name, but we're tracing the cousin who sent the preserves."

"Have you found the gun?"

"Not yet. We also checked the doors to the building and found them locked and intact."

"Well, you seem to be on the right track." Stanwick leaned forward as his meal was put before him. "Of course, knowing who the murderer is will help focus your investigation. Need I tell you?"

Who is the murderer?

Solution on page 94.

The Coolidge Letter

"EXCELLENT TEA, CATHY," remarked Thomas P. Stanwick to Catherine Weymouth, the curator of the Royston Historical Society museum. They were conversing in her office early one Wednesday afternoon.

"Thanks, Tom." She smiled. "I'm sure you'll enjoy our temporary Lincoln exhibit this summer."

"It sounds great, and will complement your other Presidential papers."

"Yes. We have a handwritten letter from Coolidge and another from Kennedy on permanent display. And a Ford in storage. But no Lincolns."

An alarm suddenly went off. Weymouth and Stanwick sprang up just as Tom Horsky, the museum security chief, rushed by.

"It's in the Goodhue Room," he called out in passing.

"Our theft alarms have a sixty-second delay," said Weymouth as she and Stanwick hurried down the hall. "But the doors lock automatically when one goes off, so the thief must still be inside."

A moment later they joined Horsky in the Goodhue Room,

which had several display cabinets. Horsky pointed to one.

"The Coolidge letter is gone," he said. "I saw it here this morning. The glass is intact and the cabinet door is closed, so the lock must have been picked."

"All right." Weymouth's mouth was a grim line. "Call the police, and bring everyone in the building to the conference room."

Three visitors were in the museum when the alarm sounded. Weymouth and Stanwick soon joined them in the conference room. The visitors agreed to be searched, and yielded up an assortment of keys, wallets, handkerchiefs, combs, coins, and pens.

"Thank you all for cooperating," Weymouth said. "A letter from President Coolidge is missing, and you were the only visitors here at the time. My security chief is gathering evidence. While we wait for the police, please tell me who you are and why you are here."

"My name's Ken Newell," said a young man with a brown goatee. "I'm working on my dissertation. Since it requires research in several old almanacs you have, I find this a convenient place to work." In addition to the almanacs, Newell had a briefcase with photocopies of text notes and a long legal pad with writing on the top sheet.

"What information in the almanacs do you use?" asked Weymouth.

"Agricultural statistics. For my thesis, I have to average out their figures on crop yields." He displayed his legal pad, which showed a long list of crops and a number beside each in a column marked "Average."

"Very interesting," said Stanwick. "What's your field of study, Mr. Newell? Economics? Math? History?"

"History."

Weymouth turned to the only other woman in the room. "And who are you, please?"

"I'm Doris Badloss, an historian and biographer," the woman replied. She had a flushed face and short, graying hair. "I was in another room, researching the life of Josiah Taylor, a colonial governor. Although I heard the alarm, I ignored it until your guard summoned me here." She had a knapsack with five books, some typed manuscript pages, a laptop computer, and bundled index cards with her.

"I see you have several reference books with you," said Weymouth.

"Yes, I brought my own."

"Sir?" Weymouth smiled at a man in his sixties with a gray suit. His effects included a hotel key and a cellular telephone.

"George Bean. Not a scholar, just a visitor. I'm in town on business—I work for an electronics company in California—and decided to spend a spare afternoon indulging my interest in history."

"Have you been to Royston before?" asked Stanwick.

"Yes, for a technology convention or two, but this is my first visit to the museum."

Horsky appeared in the doorway and beckoned to Weymouth.

"I found the letter stuck behind the cabinet," he reported. "I also found a small lockpick there. I checked the trash bins, which contained only tissues and candy wrappers. The police have just arrived."

"Wonderful!" Weymouth turned to the three visitors. "Thank you all for your patience. The police are here, so please stay here for further questioning."

She and Stanwick returned briefly to her office.

"I'm sorry your tea has gotten cold, Tom," she said teasingly.

"I'll forgive you this time," replied Stanwick with a smile, "in exchange for this little mystery. Apparently the thief got spooked by the delayed alarm. It's interesting that a Coolidge letter should be grabbed. Though he's an underrated President, I wouldn't think his papers would fetch much."

"More than you might think," said Weymouth. "The letter was handwritten, and he almost never wrote by hand when he was President. There's a black market for such papers."

"I see." Stanwick sat back and fingered the tip of his droopy mustache. "Maybe you'll lift a fingerprint off the letter, though the thief probably handled it with a handkerchief. Nonetheless, I think one of our visitors has a false alibi, and is therefore the thief."

Who tried to steal the Coolidge letter?

Solution on page 94.

The Church Supper Puzzle

"EXCELLENT HAM!" exclaimed Jerry Whalen.

"It is indeed," replied Thomas P. Stanwick as he helped himself to another slice.

It was a Saturday evening in July, and the annual Baskerville Congregational Church supper was in full swing. The light green walls of the basement framed the rows of communal tables, which were protected by lightly striped paper and piled with large serving plates of ham, baked beans, peas, rolls, corn on the cob, potato salad, and garden salad. Pitchers of coffee, iced tea, and lemonade were within the reach of all, and a crew of volunteers was already sorting the freshly baked apple, cherry, lemon meringue, blueberry, and pecan pies brought for dessert.

Among those sharing a table with Stanwick were his elderly friends Ron and Gen Hardis, Hal and Kris Hilberg with their boy Timmy, Hazel Whalen, and Hazel's middle-aged nephew, Jerry, who was visiting from the Carolinas.

"You should listen to Jerry when he talks about hams," Hazel said proudly. "It's his business, you know."

"Really?" asked Stanwick. "What do you do, Jerry?"

"I'm a sales agent for the Heckuva Honeyham company," Jerry replied, "and I'm serious about this ham. It has an unusually good glaze flavoring. Does anyone know who made it? I might make an offer for the recipe."

"Well, let's see." Stanwick leaned back in his chair and looked around. "I helped prepare the serving plates and, as I recall, the ham and most of the other food at our table were prepared by Alison, Barry, and Charlotte, who are sitting across the room. Don't know which did the ham, though."

"I was helping too," said Ron Hardis. "Alison either did the ham or baked the cherry pie, but not both."

"I was chatting with Charlotte and Barry a little while ago," added Gen. "I don't remember details, but if Barry brought either the corn on the cob or the potato salad, then Charlotte brought neither the ham nor the garden salad."

Stanwick's eyes twinkled as he finished a helping of potato salad.

"How about you, Hal? Kris?" he asked. "Any clues to our culinary mystery?"

"All I can say for sure," replied Hal with a frown, "is that either Charlotte brought the garden salad or Barry definitely did not bring the potato salad."

"We seem to be getting away from the ham," remarked Kris. "If Charlotte didn't bring it, then she brought the baked beans instead."

Ron scratched his square chin.

"I'm starting to remember better now," he said. "Either Barry brought the potato salad or Alison baked the cherry pie."

"Why, I'm starting to remember better now, too," Gen exclaimed. "Either Alison brought the ham or Charlotte brought something other than baked beans."

Timmy Hilberg had been squirming in his seat during this conversation. At last he piped up. "Can I make a suggestion? Why don't we ask them?"

"From the mouths of—well, boys," laughed Stanwick. "Quite right, Timmy. We should ask, at least to verify who baked the ham. If our collective recollections are correct, however, I've already deduced who that talented cook is."

Who baked the ham?

Solution on page 95.

The Case of the Farm Fatality

THREE MEN SAT around the kitchen table in the Borden farm-house that afternoon in late April. With John Borden were William Ryan, chief of the Baskerville police, and Thomas P. Stanwick, the amateur logician. Officer Wetherbee of the Baskerville police stood near the kitchen door.

"Rigg had had a grudge against me for a while," said Borden, a tall, lean farmer with a furrowed face and sharp, gray eyes. He was in his mid-fifties and wore a plaid shirt and blue-jean overalls. "But he was a good hand, and I kept him on because I needed his help, at least through the spring."

"Why did he have a grudge against you?" asked Stanwick.

"Well, he'd been paying attention to my daughter Elizabeth, and I didn't like it. She wants to study medicine, and I thought she could do better in choosing a fellow."

"And this morning, John? Once more, please," said Ryan quietly.

Borden paused a moment and frowned.

"I was digging a fence furrow by the outer pasture," he stated. "Some of my cows have been wandering out that way. It was about ten-thirty. Rigg snuck up behind me, from the direction of the barn. Luckily I saw his shadow, with the upraised knife. I spun around and got him first with the shovel. Pure self-defense."

"And then?" asked Ryan.

"Once I saw he was laid out, I ran back here and called it in. Nothing else to tell, really."

"In that case, if you'll excuse me, chief," said Stanwick, standing up, "I think I'll take another stroll out to the pasture."

"Go ahead, Tom," said Ryan. "I'll join you there shortly."

A few minutes later, Stanwick stood where the body of Steven Rigg had lain. After pausing to gaze north at Mount Blylock, Stanwick swept his eyes over the area. The barn was a few hundred yards to his left, and to his right lay bramble fields and woods. By his feet, the unfinished fence furrow ran toward the distant mountain. As Stanwick squatted and peered at the grass to look for signs of a struggle, Ryan came up to him.

"I left Borden with Wetherbee," Ryan said. "Anything more here?"

"I'm not sure," said Stanwick, standing up. "You know, I thought farmers dug post holes rather than trenches for fences."

"Some use the trench method, especially around here." Ryan scratched his chin solemnly. "You know, I had a report once of a quarrel between Borden and Rigg when they were in town getting cattle feed. It was nothing serious, as I recall. I sure hope this wasn't deliberate, Tom. The Bordens have farmed this land for generations."

"I know. I buy corn at their farmstand every summer. Let's see, now. I was inside all morning, and was napping when you phoned me about this. When did these clouds roll in?"

"About noon."

"Now, the side of Rigg's head was crushed in. Is that consistent with being hit by a shovel in the way Borden describes?"

"The doc thinks so. Of course, there'll be an autopsy. We've impounded the shovel in the meantime."

"That's a point for Borden, anyway. And a knife with Rigg's fingerprints was found by the body. Could that have been planted on him?"

"Can't say just yet." Ryan's face was gray.

Stanwick took a long breath, sighed, and looked again at distant Blylock.

"Well, Bill, I think it was. I hate to say this, but Borden is lying. This was a deliberate murder."

How does Stanwick know Borden is lying?

Solution on page 95.

Solutions

The Case of the Suspicious Fire (page 7)—Walker noticed that James had brown hair (which matched the beard of the man seen nearby). A man with dark hair and a smooth face at three in the morning must have shaved recently, which James would not have stopped to do had he thrown some clothes on and rushed to the scene.

The police and arson squad investigation revealed that James was indeed the bearded man. He had shaved to get a closer fit for his false beard. After removing the panel and fraying some wires to start the fire, he had walked to his car a few blocks away and driven to a bar, where he checked his message by phone until he found the message left by Henning. He then removed his beard and changed his clothes in his car, carefully washing the beard glue from his face with a solvent, before timing his arrival at the fire.

Some Trouble at Harrigan's (page 11)—Lasketter had stood in the doorway of the office and announced that the safe had been opened and the cash tray stolen. The door of the safe was open toward him, however, which would have blocked his view of the interior of the safe. He could not therefore have known that the cash tray had been taken unless he had taken it himself.

An Evening with the Logic Club (page 13)—No blue-eyed member can have a pierced ear (because he would both recite a poem and sing a song at the first meeting), and no red-headed member could have black eyes (because he would recite an essay and play the banjo at the second meeting.) Only those rules could present a contradiction to a member. Hence Arnold's deduction: green or brown eyes would cause no such problem.

Since members do not change hair or eye color, Marta could never have been a black-eyed redhead. She must therefore have blue eyes and be considering piercing her ear. Tucker (and Stanwick) deduced this and correctly surmised that Marta would contemplate taking this drastic expulsory step only if she had received or was expecting a valuable earring, probably for a major birthday or anniversary.

The River War Robbery (page 16)—The dinner celebrating Churchill's birthday on the night of the theft would have been on or around November 30. The weather a few days later, when Stanwick and Ryan were chatting, was "unusually mild" for December (but still required the use of a jacket).

For obvious climatic reasons, no tomato festival would be held in Wisconsin in December. Stanwick therefore knew that Grecco's alibi was a lie.

Murder in the Gallery (page 19)—Prichard remarked that Rosenthal probably still kept his beard trim. This implied that Rosenthal had worn a beard the last time they saw each other, which according to Rosenthal was at a high school reunion twenty years earlier. Since Rosenthal was 58, he would have been 38 then and still an officer in the Marines. Marine officers do not wear beards. Prichard must therefore have seen him more recently.

Prichard, who had nursed a grudge against Rosenthal since high school, went to the gallery first and recognized Rosenthal by his cap. After killing him, Prichard washed up and changed his shirt in the men's room, hid the bloody shirt and knife in his car, and slipped back to the pub.

The Harland Avenue Syndicate (page 23)—Debra Hassey is the killer.

The weary Walker failed to notice that if the backup thug was either Mears or Higgins, but was not Mears, he had to be Higgins. The prison legal aid expert, who served nine years, was not the arsonist, who served six years. Since the arsonist was neither the prison drug runner nor the prison tunnel digger, he must have been the prison "enforcer," who was Sullivan.

Sullivan, both arsonist and prison "enforcer," served six years. The longest term, twelve years, was served not by the legal aid expert (nine years) or by the drug runner, and so was served by the tunnel digger. This leaves the prison drug runner as the one who served three years. This was Mears, who served half as long as Sullivan. The tunnel digger was not

Hassey, and was therefore Higgins. Hassey by elimination was the legal aid expert, and served nine years.

Hassey, the prison legal aid expert, is not the driver (who knows nothing of legal aid) or the arsonist (the prison "enforcer," Sullivan) or the backup thug (the prison tunnel digger, Higgins). She is therefore the killer. Mears by elimination is the driver.

The Case of the Forged Will (page 27)—Stanwick and Bodwin both noticed that the writer of the slip of paper, who presumably was the forger, had written the date (the 11th of February, 2001, as stated in the forged will) in the Month/Day/Year format. A Briton, especially someone impersonating another Briton, would have written the date in the Day/Month/Year format, or 11/2/01. This eliminated Barbara Teti, the only British beneficiary, as a suspect.

The other two suspects were Americans, and the Month/Day/Year format is customary among most Americans. In the military, however, the Day/Month/Year format is the standard. The only beneficiary who would automatically use the Month/Day/Year format was therefore the non-military American: John Manning. Bodwin realized that the format implicated the American suspects, but Stanwick deduced that it implicated Manning specifically.

The Fainting Trader (page 31)—"In high school, I had a wonderful French teacher named Mrs. Lewis," Stanwick told Walker with a laugh. "She helped us learn by using puns. One was that 'in England, people eat two eggs for breakfast, but in France, 'one egg' is 'un oeuf.'"

"What are you talking about?" cried Walker.

"Don't you see? Montbleu is French. When he groggily came out of his initial faint, he reverted naturally to his native language. In response to your question of what was stolen, he didn't say 'enough,' he said 'un oeuf,' which is French for 'an egg.' So one of the jeweled eggs was stolen. And which of the partners had a collection of jeweled eggs? Roy Monroe. *Voila tout!*"

Stanwick and the Living Lawnmower (page 35)—Since the sheep, which eats half an acre per day, would need four days to trim Bredon's yard, the yard must be two acres in size. The bull, which eats an acre a day, would need two days to do the job, and the mule, at a quarter-acre per day, would need eight days.

The bull and the sheep together would eat 1½ acres on the first day and the remaining half-acre on the second day. Since the bull eats twice as fast as the sheep, he would eat ⅔ of the half-acre, or ⅓ acre, which would take him ⅓ day. In that ⅓ day the sheep would eat the remaining ⅙ acre.

By similar reasoning, the bull and the mule would eat 1¼ acres on the first day and the remaining ¾ acre in ⅗ of the second day. The sheep and the mule would eat ¾ acre on each of the first two days and the remaining half-acre in ⅔ of a third day. All three animals eating together would eat 1¾ acres on the first day and the remaining ¼ acre in 1⁄7 of the second day.

Bredon wants a combination that will accomplish the job in less than two days but more than 1½ days. The only combination that would do this is the bull and the mule, which would need 1 and ⅗ days.

The Adventure of the Speckled Strap (page 37)—Velma knew that Ethel had been trying on a dress when she was attacked. How could she have known this? Walker had not said so. Schweppe's was famous for its pants selection, and Ethel at least sometimes wore pants: she had worn a pair into the store (and left them on the fitting room bench when she tried on the tagged black dress). Nor had the two women supposedly spoken recently enough to discuss Ethel's shopping trip. Velma must have been there and lied about it.

Stanwick and Walker learned that the flirtatious Ethel had caused her friend Velma's engagement to break up years earlier. Velma had ostensibly remained Ethel's friend while planning her revenge. That day Velma had followed Ethel and slipped into the fitting room while Ethel was at the mirror around the corner of the hut. Upon Ethel's return to the room, Velma had surprised her and strangled her with a strap from a discarded dress.

The Frequent Flier from Rio (page 40)—Based on the assumptions that a) Gandolfo gets the skins onto the plane at Rio, b) he does not bring the skins off the plane himself, but c) regains possession of the skins quickly once he is in the city, Stanwick hypothesized that Gandolfo paid a confederate to take the skins off the plane for him.

Who could it be? Not one of the other passengers, who are also thoroughly searched. Nor could it be one of the flight crew, for the reasons Cooper gave. Stanwick realized, however, that the airport authority had to employ a local crew to clean and tidy up the interior of the plane between its arrival at Royston and its departure for Rio the next day.

It would be fairly simple for Gandolfo to bring the package aboard in his briefcase, hide it under his seat or in the magazine pocket (especially since he had no seating companion) and have an accomplice on the cleaning crew retrieve the package for him. The accomplice could conceal the package in his cleaning cart and not have to go through Customs. He could then meet Gandolfo in the city, hand over the package, and get paid. This proved to be so.

Death of a Rye Writer (page 43)—McCourt's compulsive work habits enabled Stanwick to deduce when he was murdered.

The writer started work on a new manuscript on Monday the 5th and produced two pages an hour for eight hours a day, six days a week. If he had been alive at 10 A.M. on the 23rd, as his daughter claimed, he would have produced at least 260 pages of manuscript. (Sixteen working days through the 22nd at eight hours per day are 128 hours; another two hours on the morning of the 23rd make 130 hours, and two pages per hour make 260 pages.) He was only up to page 250 in his typewriter, however, which implied that he had been murdered five working hours earlier, or at 11 P.M. the night before. His daughter was therefore lying when she said she saw him alive that morning, which points to her as the murderer.

Ann Kitchens was struggling as a playwright and too eager to inherit her father's estate. She visited him in his study on the evening of the 22nd, murdered him, pulled up the window shade to back up her story about seeing him alive the next morning, and disposed of the needle in town.

Theft in a Knordwyn Shop (page 46)—Sweeney is the thief.

Since the three visited the shop at different times, only one could have taken the bag. Snow's second statement that, in effect, he and Sweeney are not both guilty must therefore be true. Snow is therefore a truthteller, so his first statement is also true. Since this statement contradicts Speakman's first statement, she is a liar, and since Sweeney says she is right, he is also a liar. His second statement is therefore false, so he is the thief.

Speakman must have stolen something sometime in her life, but not this time!

The Talk of the Pub (page 49)—Stanwick knew that no consistent liar would admit to being a liar, which would be telling the truth. Mangone therefore lied when he said Cormier admitted being a liar. Since Mangone, a liar, said Cormier was a liar, Cormier must be a truthteller.

Stanwick could then piece together the conversation in logical order. Squire Cronin had truthfully said he would leave all his money to one of the two charity heads, but only to someone who visited him at home. All visitors to his home had to pat his pets on the head (the contradictory of the lying Mangone's first statement). These pets included a llama, a woolly animal.

Harry Kinsley is allergic to wool, and so would not pat a llama. He could therefore never have visited the squire at the squire's home, since then either (a) he would not strictly avoid all allergy-provoking animals, which would mean a truthteller (Glynn) had made a false statement, or (b) the squire did not require all visitors to pat his pets on the head, which would mean a liar (Mangone) had made a true statement. Kinsley would therefore not get the squire's money. Since the money is to go either to him or to Ruth Segal, it will thus go to Ruth.

The Case of the Kidnapped Consultant (page 51)—The use of the garage access code by the kidnappers indicated the likely involvement of someone in the building, most likely an associate of the kidnapped man.

Kvicala's assumption that ransom had been demanded was reasonable. Stanwick was struck, however, by Harding's inquiry about Russell's car. It would have been quite a leap for an innocent man to infer that the kidnappers, despite using the garage elevator, had taken the victim's own car to escape. Kidnappers usually provide their own transportation. Since Harding no longer used the garage himself, he would not simply have noticed the absence of Russell's car when he arrived for work.

Harding therefore knew that the kidnappers had used Russell's car, and in seeking to appear ignorant but concerned, he let this knowledge slip out. Stanwick therefore suspected his complicity, which Bodwin's investigation subsequently confirmed.

A Shocking Christmas (page 55)—If the husband or daughter are assumed to be innocent and truthful, then one of the three visiting neighbors must have been out of sight and earshot of the family members for some period after arriving that evening. The only visitor unaccounted for after arriving but before Mary's death was Brady, whose whereabouts from a quarter to eight until eight were not verified by the presence of a family member. She had been in the living room from seven-thirty, when she arrived, until a quarter to eight, but at eight she had "returned" to the living room. Returned from where?

Brady altered the toy village circuitry in the dining room between a quarter to eight and eight, and moved the meeting house so that Mary would be likely to touch it. The developer's money was too tempting.

The Secret Scholarships (page 59)— Since Roger is applying for the Ridgway and Brian is not applying for the Tavorkian, Brian is applying for the Dickinson. Russ by elimination must be applying for the Tavorkian, which is therefore in history. The Dickinson is not in math, so it must be the chemistry scholarship. This leaves the Ridgway as the math scholarship.

In summary: Roger is applying for the Ridgway in math, Brian is applying for the Dickinson in chemistry, and Russ is applying for the Tavorkian in history.

Stanwick and the Stolen Bonds (page 61)—The thief had to know about the bonds and the hidden key, which restricts the suspect list to Greeley and Fabiano. Fabiano, a small man, could not have reached the six-foot shelf easily enough to saw off the padlock and reach inside. Nor was there any furniture in the basement, or small, moveable furniture upstairs, that he could have used to stand on.

The thief was therefore Greeley. He had stolen the bonds before going to the mall that day.

A Minivan Mystery (page 65)—The license plate on the killer's van was genuine, but not in the state database. Stanwick realized that the number, N68SXH, could have been produced by turning upside-down a plate numbered HXS89N. When that plate number turned out to belong to Caponette, he was conclusively implicated.

Caponette and Levine were both involved in a prescription drug ring and had quarreled over the money. Caponette then stalked Levine for several weeks to learn her routine, including her weekly skating session. Just before the murder, he inverted his license plate as a precaution.

The Impossible Poisoning (page 68)—The evidence did not rule out one alternative means of transmitting the poison orally: toothpaste.

Fred Mettler's morning washup routine would have included brushing his teeth. Sandy Mettler injected poison into the toothpaste tube at home, and Fred ingested it orally when he brushed, either by swallowing a tiny quantity of it or through a small cut in his mouth. Since Sandy shared the small house but avoided the poisoned tube, she presumably prepared it. Walker's investigation confirmed this.

A Carlie Conundrum (page 71)—The children are 8, 10, 14, and some age over 14 but below 20. If Charlie's child were 10 or older, then Joanie's, who is twice as old, would have to be at least 20, which is impossible. Therefore Charlie's child is 8 and Joanie's is 16.

Helen's son is not Jimmy, who is Bob's son, so her son is Andrew. Since Andrew is at a Disney site, he is not the 14-year-old visiting Cleveland. Andrew is therefore the 10-year-old at Disneyland. The 14-year-old is Bob's son, Jimmy.

Since Joanie is not visiting either Disney site or Cleveland (where Bob and Jimmy are), she must be with Alison at the Grand Canyon. Charlie by elimination must be with Tanisha at Disney World.

In summary: Charlie and Tanisha (age 8) are at Disney World, Helen and Andrew (age 10) are at Disneyland, Bob and Jimmy (age 14) are in Cleveland, and Joanie and Alison (age 16) are at the Grand Canyon.

Lunch at the Quill & Truncheon (page 74)—Since Sumner had asthma, Stanwick knew that he would not have lunched regularly in a pub with a confined, smoky atmosphere like the Quill & Truncheon. Meyers was therefore lying about his friendly relationship with Sumner in order to cover up his murderous reason for calling on the man who, as Bodwin later proved, had been blackmailing him. Sumner had let him in expecting a payment, and instead received a bullet.

The Coolidge Letter (page 78)— Newell was the thief. He had no calculator.

He said he was averaging crop statistics from several almanacs, and showed a resulting list of crops and their averages. If this was so, how did he calculate the averages? He had no calculator. He had no computer. Neither his papers nor the trash cans contained scratch paper with figures. Had he been so gifted mathematically as to average several large numbers in his head, he probably would have been pursuing his degree in mathematics. Stanwick's questions excluded this possibility.

His alibi was therefore false, prepared to explain his presence in the museum if necessary. He extracted the Coolidge letter to sell it on the black market, but hid it on hearing the alarm.

The Church Supper Puzzle (page 81)—If Barry brought the potato salad, then Charlotte both did (by Hal's statement) and did not (by Gen's first statement) bring the garden salad. Since this is impossible, Barry did not bring the potato salad. By Ron's second statement, Alison therefore brought the cherry pie and, by his first statement, did not bake the ham.

By Gen's second statement, since Alison did not bake the ham, Charlotte did not bring the baked beans. If Kris is correct, therefore, Charlotte must have baked the ham.

The Case of the Farm Fatality (page 84)—As Stanwick stood by the fence furrow and looked at the mountain to the north, the barn was to his left. The barn was therefore west of the furrow. Had Rigg approached Borden from the direction of the barn that morning, as Borden stated, Rigg's shadow would have been cast back toward the barn, not toward Borden. Borden was therefore lying when he said that Rigg's shadow warned him of an attack.

Index